Don't Be A Schmuck

By Michael Hofeld

First Printing Edition 2020

New Toy Media LLC
30 Clover Hill Circle
Egg Harbor Township, NJ 08234

Contents

Introduction: Always Bet on Yourself

Are you thinking of starting a business or have you already taken the leap? Betting on yourself is always a great move. Yet it's a big step to take and you want to be prepared. I'm here to help. This book is an accumulation of knowledge and anecdotes that will help you start and succeed in business. Beyond that it will assist you in figuring out what drives you and how to be happy along the way.

The goal is to help you find the best path to your success by explaining the process in a fun no nonsense way. Advice to make the right choices and expose you to some shortcuts to your goals. Also keeping you from making boneheaded moves when there are simple answers. Getting you to a place where you are happy and can make a buck. It's just that simple.

There are tons of useful pieces of wisdom in here, but even if you get just one or two that is a huge win. A single trick or tip could save you a ton of time, money, or energy. That could be the difference between success and failure in business.

This book comes straight from my heart, I did my best to not include any fluff or try to overreach in any areas I have not experienced. When I found good stories that I thought would be entertaining and benefit you I inserted them in the book. This is not about me. This is about you and discovering the best way to start a business and be happy. That's all I wish for you

You don't need to read every word front to back to benefit from the knowledge in here. If you want to take a non-traditional way of cutting to what is most important to you I have a suggestion. Read the "final words" of each chapter first. If they interest you, go back and read the entire chapter. As I often say, there is no one path to knowledge.

You might wonder, why call the book Don't Be a Schmuck? From an early age I was taught how to make a profit. Taught this by my father and others who were mostly from the old school of business. When I would make a mistake they would say don't be a schmuck. This mistake was so plain to them and they would correct me. Don't be a schmuck, do this instead. In the back of my mind there has always been that voice guiding me during my many startups. Hence it is a tongue and cheek way for me to teach people and pay homage to my past.

Throughout the book you will find little pieces of fortune cookie wisdom labeled DBAS. This stands for Don't Be a Schmuck. If you don't know, schmuck is a word that means moron or asshole. These tips are meant to encapsulate some of the most important or simplest lessons.

Schmuck may sound like a nasty word but in the situation it's a term of endearment. It is said with love. Because I love you, I don't want you to do something stupid. So, don't be a schmuck read this book make money and be happy.

Chapter 1: Should You Start Your Own Business

Looks like you are considering embarking on the journey of a lifetime. Starting your own business can fulfill your lifelong dreams, while utilizing all your amazing talents. What an exciting time for you. Before you take the great leap let me pass along some hard learned lessons to help make the path just a tad bit easier.

Let's start with a simple question, should you start your own business? Is it part of your or human fabric? The goal of this book is to see if starting your own business is a good idea and then what to do next. I'll take the 40 years that I've been in the entrepreneurship game and pass the nuggets that I've learned along to you. My goal is to make sure you are not a schmuck. Saving you time, money, and energy. Yet that knowledge isn't of value unless owning your own business is right for you. Let us begin.

The New American Dream

Startups have become the new American dream. At one point the goal was the picket fence, the house, two kids, and a car. Then it morphed to just wealth, like winning Powerball or the lottery. The form it has taken now is that of being a startup king or queen. Starting Facebook, Instagram, Uber, or Airbnb and becoming a billionaire through your own brilliance. Entrepreneurship has been here forever but we're living in a different age. Where masters of this arena have become the new rock stars of the world. These are not necessarily power magnets of the past, the Rockefellers or JP Morgan. It's not that same type of business landscape, where it's a massive undertaking that requires thousands of people and large capital investment to start. Now just an idea can change the world. This is the dream which drives many to start their own companies.

When determining whether being an entrepreneur is part of your soul, one of the first questions I would ask is how long have you been thinking about starting your own business?

Has it been a day, a week, a month, a year or longer? If you have been thinking about it a long time, has the idea evolved? Why haven't you done anything about it yet? If this is just a passing fancy it might be a bad idea. If this is something that has been burning inside, then it deserves further investigation.

Have you had a trial run?

Something else that is telling about your proclivity to be an entrepreneur is if you have ever started a business of any size? Did you run your own lemonade stand? Did you sell t-shirts? Buy stuff at garage sales? Sell your old collectibles on eBay?

Have you ever had your own business where the goal was turning a profit? For some people that hustle has been there their whole life and is just waiting to be unleashed in a more formal fashion.

Understanding what goes into operating a business, what the costs would be, running into unexpected things, the joy of making a profit are a big part of being an entrepreneur. So, any experience that you have had running a business would benefit you going forward. If somehow you have never hustled to make an extra dollar you should ask yourself, why not?

Is there an idea for a business or is business the idea?

I would also ask do you have an idea that has coalesced already or do you just feel "I want to start my own business but I don't know what". If you have an idea, how much research have you done? It may be putting the cart before the horse a little bit. If you've done research great, if you haven't it's a good way to build your idea.

Have you investigated competing companies? Looked into the news and industries regarding it? That's from a more global perspective, on a local level it's more about just taking note of how the market is around you, the economy in your area. Is there saturation for a particular product? If you want to open up a pizza place, are there already 30 pizza restaurants where you live?

Is it in your blood?

Certain people are born and bred to be entrepreneurs. Are you one of them? Is anybody in your family an entrepreneur or anybody close to you? The reason that I ask is because a lot of what I've learned came from my father. In my eyes an outstanding entrepreneur who had his own men's clothing business.

Yet he didn't learn from his father, but from a group of sharp businessmen including a Holocaust survivor named Warner Bing. Entrepreneurship is often passed down from person to person. Not necessarily from family to family but by somebody who can be your guiding light, a mentor. This isn't as important as it used to be now we have the internet to help and books like this. The idea of this book is to be a version of Obie Wan to steer you away from the rough waters and to get you to the calm seas. Like the mentors I have had in my career.

Have You Been Witness?

Yet, if you have been around people who own their own business you will have learned a significant amount without even trying. Through osmosis. Having witnessed how a startup or a small business can impact a person. I think it's valuable if your mother, your father's sister, your brother, anybody close to you has run their own business. Successfully or unsuccessfully, it doesn't matter, you can learn either way.

The more exposure that you have to entrepreneurship, the more likely you are to understand whether it's inside of you. That's a little bit of a holistic way of looking at something, but the truth is that succeeding in business is not going to always be about numbers or having the right answer. A lot of it is going to be about feelings. To know yourself and to know what you're getting into.

If I sound like somebody who is standing in the gateway and being wary of whether you should enter, I am. Being a business owner is not for everyone. Actually it is for the very few.

Are you @#%&! crazy?

In my own life anytime someone asks me whether I think it's a good idea whether they should start their own business, my one question is simple, "Are you fucking crazy?"

When I ask, "Are you crazy?", they look at me in shock. They don't understand the question because they think that I'm impugning their idea. No, what I really mean is are you abnormal? Are you off-kilter? Are you unusual? Because starting a company and being an entrepreneur does not subscribe to any sort of format you're going to see anywhere else. Every day is a new adventure and you must be a little screwed in the head to do it.

The people who I have seen create the best startups are the most screwed up. For one reason or another they have a chip on their shoulder or just look at the world differently. If you are a by the book, standard person who wants a simple life I totally respect that. Entrepreneurship is all I know. It's all I can do. Some days I wish I could just decide to have a nine to five job. Make a nice living, go home, have a wife, a couple of kids and be happy. But that is not me. I am driven by entrepreneurship and yes, I am definitely crazy.

You must ask yourself, are you fucking crazy? And I mean that in the nicest possible way. Some of the most interesting and fun people you ever meet are a little bit crazy. And that's what it's going to take to be an entrepreneur. Are you crazy? ARE YOU FUCKING CRAZY? Answer that question for yourself. If the answer is yes, then you should move forward. If the answer is no, you are either lying to yourself or you might want to turn back before it's too late. ☺

DBAS: Running your own business isn't for everyone.

Silicon Valley Doesn't = The World

Talking about whether this is for you or not, I want to separate the real world from the Silicon Valley culture. Startups have become the worldwide dream of coming up with the unique idea that makes you a billionaire. That's not what I think startups are really about. What has happened in Silicon Valley is that whole culture is about valuations and building paper wealth. Businesses that work at their core are not at a premium. Profit isn't the goal. Return on investment drives motives.

This book is about creating a business that turns a profit, that can scale and be the vessel for your happiness. Whether you want to sell it, go public or pass it on to your kids. We're focusing on building a sound foundation.

A lot of what you'll see in Silicon Valley is darts at a wall. Venture capital puts 10 million dollars in 100 different ventures. Investing a billion dollars and expecting to get $5 billion back. Planning that one of the 100 companies is going to hit big. What you find with venture capital is often they would rather you fail than be a medium success.

We're not going to talk much about that type of strategy. Let's focus on building your business on solid fundamentals. Something that you can get your arms around and continue to grow from year to year. Don't worry we aren't ruling out those massive windfall of cash. If you catch lightning in a bottle the money will be there, but that isn't the way to approach a business from the outset. For now, let's put them out of our mind in order to build something that reflects your goals and passion.

Final Words:

Take stock of how much entrepreneurship has been in your life up until this point. Is there an idea burning inside of you? Have you been surrounded by people who run their own businesses? Are you abnormal enough to make this work?

We are at the beginning of getting you to where you want to go. Keep an open mind and be able to look yourself in the mirror to see who you truly are.

Chapter 2: Very Brief History of My Entrepreneurial Journey

Our goal, I spoke of in the first chapter is trying to determine whether being an entrepreneur is in you. Is it who you are? Where is it, buried under something and we just need to dust it off to find that diamond in the rough? Here is a quick explanation of my journey, it might help. You can get a sense of how I've become the man I am today, by being an entrepreneur my whole life.

The Family Business

I mentioned in the first chapter that I come from a family that owned a men's clothing store in Atlantic City, New Jersey. I learned from both my mother and father how you run a business. Every night at dinner my father would come home and teach me some sort of lesson. This could be about accounting, employee relations, markup, margin, advertising, etc. It wasn't like he meant to do it, but he needed someone to vent. I was his audience who found these topics fascinating.

After a few years in the clothing business my father worked his way up to become a wholesale salesman for a factory. During his time selling to shopkeepers he met a man in one store at Fort Dix in New Jersey named Werner Bing (a Holocaust survivor by the way). Werner taught him how to be a merchant, how to buy, sell and make money.

Along with what he had learned in the clothing industry since age 15 my pops had enough gumption to start his own business. The company started was in 1977 and was open until 2010 when my parents retired.

That is my lineage of being an entrepreneur. Werner Bing to my dad to me.

Old World Smarts

As fate would have it, when Werner retired from his shop, he opened up a concession inside my father's clothing store selling shoes. As a child I worked alongside both of them doing simple tasks. But they were teaching me and engraining me with the spirit of an entrepreneur without me even knowing it.

Let me give you a small window into the old-world logic that I was able absorb. One year it was springtime and the temperature started to get warm earlier than usual. When I arrived at the store, I found my dad back in the tailor shop. Having a tailor shop on premises made it easy for customers to get their clothing fitted, fast and cheap. But it served another purpose on this day because my father was in there making a commotion. All I saw was fabric all over the floor, it looked like he went crazy... crazy like a fox. What he had done was cut up the long sleeve shirts from the winter and put a nice hem in them. Instantly turned them into short sleeved shirts.

I know that sounds so basic and simple, but most methods of making money aren't rocket science. He showed me, don't overcomplicate it. Our spring inventory hadn't come in yet, but it's warm outside, let's cut the sleeves off and make some money. I love that story and I think about it often when confronted with a problem in enterprises. Sometimes you get overwhelmed by a challenge. You just need to look at the simplest path to making money with what you have and do it. Stop overthinking.

DBAS: Making money isn't always complicated. Simple solutions can yield amazing profits.

From the Tiniest Acorn

Start with my first business at 10 years old. This was going to a little candy store around the corner from my house and bringing the sweets to school to resell. I would open shop for other kids at lunchtime or before school. I would double my money making 20 bucks a day. That's a fricking fortune to a 10-year-old in 1983. This is when I got hooked on running my own business. The rush of making a profit while providing a much-needed service made me feel like a king. Crowds of kids surrounding me to get their confections. I would continue to chase that feeling for the rest of my life.

You Get a Stick of Gum and an Education

Even at the earliest age, I was always trying to figure out a hustle and how to make money. After I got busted by the principal for selling candy, I moved big time into baseball cards in the mid-80s. I built a nice business off of buying and selling them. Trying to identify cards that would become in demand in the future was a challenge that I excelled at. I had to handicap players and how they would perform in upcoming seasons. The better a player performed the higher the price would go.

Also, I had to evaluate scarcity, some cards were easy to find while some others were like gold dust. I quickly learned that people always want what they couldn't have.

So, I specialized in the hard to find cards. This venture helped continue to build my business toolbox and lasted till I was 16. I recognized that the market had become oversaturated. The real money was gone and I began selling off the majority of my collection as prices peaked over the next few years.

Mini Entrepreneur

My next stage of development was when I was in high school. I sold custom printed T-shirts for different events. This was way before it was easy to have T-shirts made like today. Now you just go on Vistaprint and boom. Using connections from my parents clothing store, I found printers and designers. The sales were done hand to hand with my first business partner, a fella named Andrew Loggi. Someone who I ended up working with for 20 years thereafter. Selling T-shirts was about being witty with designs and knowing your customer. I also learned that it's a monkey see monkey do world. If a few of the more popular kids got some of our designs, the rest of the school would fall in line. This business kept me flush with cash till almost graduation.

Then in college I ran into an old friend of the family who owned some local free newspapers for tourists. He had known me since I was 7 years old and found me to be ambitious and aggressive. I took over one of his publications. I ran my own newspaper at 18, which had a circulation of about ten thousand a week. I ran that for a couple of years. Learning about selling advertising, the importance of distribution, value of solid creative, margins, product sourcing. Sucking it all up like a sponge.

When you're young it was just "hey I need the money for the summer". I didn't realize that I was growing into the man I would become based on these jobs. The newspaper was great because I would work 20 hours a week and make double what anybody I knew was earning. I made a thousand dollars a week as a college student, which again back then was absurd money. Working only 20 hours a week, I'd go to the beach and the movies the rest of the time. This was my introduction into a cornerstone of entrepreneurship which rewards smart work first and hard work second.

That produced my mantra: Work smart first and hard work second. Hard work is necessary, but it is way more valuable if it is done in an intelligent fashion. I did 40 hours of work in 20 hours' time.

Cubicles Aren't For Me

After the newspaper when I graduated college (Boston University's School of Management) I moved out to L.A. and I went to work for Hanna-Barbera. The creators of classic cartoons like Yogi Bear, The Jetsons, and The Flintstones. I had a degree and I went to work in their accounting department. It was pretty hard to get a job in Hollywood and I had been working every angle just to get in the door at a major entertainment company. Yet I lasted only two weeks there before I quit. At the end of the day it was still an accounting job. Even though the columns read Jetson's or Flintstone's or whatever, it was still just accounting. We had neat stuff in our office reminding us that we worked for a cartoon company, but it was boring and basic. I couldn't use all the tools that I had spent my youth learning. That was exactly the time that I knew that a corporate gig was not for me.

I didn't have the patience to spend years tinkering in one department to try to climb my way to the top. Where I could finally have my hands in everything. That's part of being an entrepreneur, you've got to be involved in all of the business. If you are curious by nature, the boundaries of a rigid corporation stunt your growth. If you're somebody who really enjoys being focused on one thing then entrepreneurship may be harder for you. Business owners need to be nimble.

After Hanna Barbera, I left LA and moved back east. I started a few ventures during that time around 1996. My favorite was where I was buying classic videogames, the standup ones from the arcades like Pac Man, Space Invaders. Then selling them to rich clientele around New York, New Jersey and Pennsylvania. That was a great idea and I had more customers than I ever expected. Yet what I learned was that the logistics of business can be awful. Delivering the machines, the upkeep, and customer service. Just because you can buy it for $100 and sell it for a $1,000 doesn't make it a good business. The amount of aggravation post sale ran me out of this venture, but I have never lost the thrill of buying something cheap and selling it for more.

Destiny Awaits

The late 90s is when the Internet came mainstream and turned commercial. Right around this time I was somewhat rudderless and by happenstance reconnected with an old boss. I don't know if you believe in fate or destiny, but I was on the street in Atlantic City looking for the human resources department at a casino to apply for a summer gig. I took a wrong turn and literally ran into the fellow who owned the tourist newspaper company. He asked me what I was up to and offered me a job on the spot.

He turned out to be another one of my mentors and his name is Craig Weintraub. He taught me a ton including how to be a good boss and to care about the right things. Within a month of working for him I pitched the idea of moving the tourist paper concept online. In 1997 we started my first web based company called Atlantic Internet Development. Designing web sites for the Jersey Shore tourists and the experience was eye opening.

You still had to have a vision of what the Internet could become, but luckily I could see it. The web was going to replace these free newspapers, not just in New Jersey, but everywhere. I went to Craig and told him I wanted to develop these types of sites all over the country. He was a mench, but knew his limitations and said "I don't know anything about everywhere else. You go and do your thing". I set out to tackle the whole world and Craig went from a 50% partner to a 5% partner.

BIG INC. goes BIG

In 1998 along with two of my best friends, I started a company called Bender Internet Group, Big Inc. which would dominate the next 15 years of my life. We built some of the earliest online travel guides. Sold hotel rooms, event tickets, and much more. For 10 years as we grew, we worked closely with Hotels.com and the guys who founded that company. I was there when Hotels.com went public on the Nasdaq and got a nice little picture of myself pressing the button at market opening. (You don't ring the bell at Nasdaq you just press the button.) We learned so much in that company, manipulating Google and other different distribution methods. Monetizing web real estate. Negotiating well above market supplier relationships.

Over time the industry matured, and the distribution channels changed dramatically. The company rose, plateaued, and declined over the course of a decade. We went through 4 acquisition attempts by major corporations but never consummated a deal. Which might be the only regret. We made a lot of money, had a lot of fun, generated a billion dollars in sales and played on the biggest stages. But all good things come to an end.

After the Show is the After Party

Businesses have lifecycles and BIG Inc found its end. Leading up to this finish I searched for new ventures to grow for the next stage of my life. I started a TV station, opened a glossy magazine (something like Maxim). Played professional poker. Produced a documentary film called Action Junkies. Constantly working on multiple projects. The biggest one was a new travel company called Reserve Vacations focusing on vacation packages.

In 2012 another growing industry caught my eye and I founded a company in the daily fantasy sports industry called Rotocasino. (Now dominated by Fanduel and Draftkings.) A lifelong sports fan, I very much enjoyed the industry, but quickly moved from being on the supply side of the business to a personality. Launching a popular podcast interviewing the biggest names in the industry. Additionally, I was the founder of the largest private championship. Attracting the best players in the world what became the most prestigious championship in daily fantasy sports. The FCK challenge.

That business taught me a lot about analytics, expected value, where to find good edges. Ultimately in business what you want to do is put a dollar in, get more back and then repeat as many times as humanly possible. Simple right?

A Kid in a Candy Store

Today, I run a handful of enterprises around digital marketing and travel. I'm involved in companies that are testing the new worlds of business including virtual reality, blockchain, big data and personalization. Yet, my favorite business is the growth consulting company. Helping companies find unique ways to expand their businesses. Working with companies of all sizes. My love of aiding people in solving the puzzle of how to make a business work never goes away. It's that same feeling I had when I started selling candy as a kid in middle school.

Final Words:

We were talking about arcade games before. When I was a kid you would go to the arcade and put a dollar in the change machine and get four quarters back. In business my goal was put a dollar in and get four quarters plus a nickel, dime or a dollar more. Then put another dollar bill in and just keep doing it all day and night. That's what I've been doing for the last 20 years. Putting it all in the money machine and trying to get more out. Sometimes the return is higher than others, but that's business.

Starting from an early age, entrepreneurship has been a part of my daily life and it's something that I couldn't or wouldn't want to escape from. It is just who I am. Through the years I have generated over five billion dollars in sales. (I wish I had figured out how to put more of that in my pocket, but more on that later).

Now, thinking about the times at Hanna-Barbera when I wanted to be in the entertainment industry because I thought it was so cool, I didn't know myself yet. I was fighting my very nature. My skillset was knowing how to make money and solve problems. I'm so glad I didn't try and convince myself to wait years to be able to prove that. That's the wonderful things about being an entrepreneur, if you believe in yourself, you can prove it almost immediately. Looking back, it feels like I never had a choice, I was born to be an entrepreneur. For better or worse.

Enough about me. Let's get more into you, whether this is for you and the best ways to go about starting your business.

Chapter 3: Business is a Risk. Are You A Risk Taker?

To thine own self be true. Knowing your style as an entrepreneur is critical. You must understand who you are to be able to pick the right path. You might think that you want to pick the path of least resistance, but the optimal path is going to depend on your personality. You must assess who you are to know the correct route . Being delusional about who you are and what you are good at is poison to the entrepreneur.

A simple test is to ask yourself, am I a gambler? Do you hate gambling or risk taking? Are you unwilling to put like $5 on bingo or bet your friend a dollar that you can throw this piece of garbage into the trash can five feet away? If you have a fear of risk, then entrepreneurship might be a little hard for you. Starting your own business is one gamble after another. Gambling is taking a risk on an uncertain outcome. It is preferable that you are somewhat comfortable with a future that is unwritten.

Place Your Bets

If you don't gamble or you haven't gambled recently, I recommend you go find a way to wager a few $. Maybe on a game of Words with Friends or on a coin toss. Money changes people's ability to perform and make decisions. So I want you to try and capture that feeling when the outcome is in the balance. One of my favorite sayings is "You can't play poker for pretzels." That if you we're sitting down with friends to play poker (but works for any game). Each of you gets a stack of pretzels to begin the game. People wouldn't really care about it if they won or lost. Pretzels have little or no value. Part of the game of poker is about risk and reward, much like business. If there is no actual risk or reward, then you aren't really playing poker.

The value of things will change your decision. So even if you're playing poker for 25 or 50 cents I guarantee you it's entirely different than if you're playing for pretzels.

Grace Under Fire

Businesses don't operate in a vacuum. A plan on a piece of paper is going to look all fine and good, but then things will change once you start up. That's the risk in all of this. Part of understanding how you'll feel under pressure. Obviously, there are plenty of tasks that you can perform where you must make decisions under duress. Whether it be playing sports, public speaking, being a parent. Many situations where you can feel pressure and feel like you must execute . Then add money to that. (If your life is on the line, it's far more severe like in the military.) Again, my goal is for you to think of a time when you had to operate with a ticking clock. Then try to analyze how this made you feel and how you responded.

I mentioned before that I spent some time in the world of professional poker. For a few years I travelled out to Las Vegas to play at the World Series of Poker. I was blessed with competing with some of the best players in the world. Playing poker was one of the finest experiences I've ever had for helping me be a better entrepreneur. The game is a microcosm of a business. You're confronted with decisions every hand, you have imperfect information and try to come up with scenarios for what's going on. Money's involved and you must understand what are people's motivations. Some people are going for it all and others are just trying to eek out a profit. Just like your competitors in business.

DBAS: Risk is part of business. How much you take is up to you. Don't take risk just for the excitement. Be methodical.

To Thine Own Self Be True

You learn in poker that you must know who you are and what's your style of play. There are some people that like to wait for the best hand, kind of like waiting for an amazing idea to come along. Something that can't miss. That's the idea that they want to go all in. Then you have other people who are wild, who just want the action. They want to be in a business, they want to be in a poker hand. They're just going to throw money around willy-nilly. They think mainly of the reward and not the risk.

The difference being is that the person who's conservative is less likely to lose money than the person who's wild. Yet, the wild person is more likely to make a lot of money quickly. Conservative players are more likely to make money over the long haul. Risk/reward exists and as a human being this is not news to you. The key is that you must understand how to balance the two for you personally. To be comfortable with the amount of risk you take on. If not, your worry will cloud your mind, and its ability to make the correct choices.

Goldy Locks the Hell Out of It

The optimal way that you can operate is what is called selective aggressiveness, which means that you're never too crazy and you're never too conservative. Where you are willing to attack when the opportunities present themselves, and you won't hesitate. Yet, when things aren't promising you aren't going to get bored, lose your patience and get involved just to feel the adrenaline. Selective aggressiveness is something that I strongly feel people should try to operate from in entrepreneurship. You must try to mitigate the downside of things, but you can't be afraid to pounce once opportunity is there for the taking.

No Way To Simulate Live Fire

Consider situations where you had to take a chance. Maybe you look at the weather forecast, and it says there's a 60% chance of rain, but you say I'll roll the dice and go to the beach anyway. What's the worst thing that can happen, I'll get wet? There are other situations where the downside can be far more severe.

 Being in business where you're putting up money in hopes of making more money is the purest form of gambling. I sat in a room where we were doing a $50 million acquisition. While we were meeting to do the due diligence, we were hit by two lawsuits from two different billion-dollar companies.

They both were trying to stop the third company from acquiring us. That moment still gives me an uneasy feeling. That was a time when the stakes got a little high for me. The thoughts racing through my head were overwhelming. We had been crushing it for years, leading up to this moment. All the hopes and dreams of the people that I worked with were on my shoulders along with my own ambitions.

I had been very aggressive in the way that I had gone about this acquisition. I had bluffed a publicly traded company into thinking we were being acquired by their largest competitor, when in fact it was a foreign investor. The deal eventually fell apart, but I had increased the sale price of our company by 10x. I would do it again tomorrow. The risk was worth the reward to me. Others in my company didn't see it the same way and it caused dissent in the years moving forward. So, you must be aware of not only your risk tolerance, but also your partners'.

Some people wouldn't be able to live with the pressure. Yes, I was overwhelmed in a singular moment but, I fought through it. This was because I knew who I was. I had no kids; no debt and I could take tons of risks. I said I would make this gamble again tomorrow, but that would be under the same circumstances. Today I'm a different person who would have to consider where I am in my life now. This is exactly what I am preaching to you. Know who you are, know what type of risks you can live with. (Alright maybe I should have just taken the $25 million and not been so greedy, but I'd probably be dead by now).

Final Words: Understand what type of risk you can live with in business. It's not wrong to be conservative. It's not wrong to be wild either. Don't go against your nature as an entrepreneur or you will have a much harder time succeeding. Commit to your style and go after it.

Chapter 4: Motivations Drive Goals

Age Before Beauty

Age and goals matter when you're thinking about starting your own business. Different people have different reasons for starting a business. I know it's not nice to say that you're too old or too young to do something. Because the truth is, you're not. Yet the likelihood of success given what age you are is a differentiating factor.

In a standard situation if you're younger you have less to lose than somebody who is older. You can operate on a leaner budget. On the flipside, people who have more experience are more likely to have a clear vision of their plan and what it takes to implement it. They have seen more, so they know more, they can do more. However, the folly of youth often is that you feel indestructible. Some of that feeling of being unbreakable is necessary for being an entrepreneur because you're doing something that you have never done before.

There are going to be naysayers. You must feel like you can't be stopped. Regardless of age, the question you need to be asking is "why are you doing this?" and "what's your end game?" What your goals are matters to whether you should start a business, whether your idea is suitable for you or the best way to go about it.

Reasons to start your own business:

- Money- Duh
- Prove Yourself – For the haters
- Personal Freedom – No alarm clock
- Job Security – You don't fire yourself
- Variety of Tasks – You will not be bored
- Self-Actualization – Namaste
- Cut Through Red Tape – No one standing in your way.

What Drives You?

In the previous chapter we talked about knowing yourself, knowing what type of risk you're comfortable with. In this chapter, it's more talking about why you are doing this. The number one reason for most people is money and obviously that is a driving factor in our society. Money buys things. It creates security and a sense of freedom. You can do things for yourself, for your spouse, for your kids or for your parents.

Money is a reason. Not the Reason.

There are studies about income that show if you make over $75,000 a year, making more money isn't going to make you happier. I know that's hard for people to come to grips with because they say "That's not me. I'll be happy. I know how to spend money to make my life better." And that's perfectly fine, but it has not been my experience that richer people are happier. Take a breath. Seriously let that sink in.

However, it has been my observation that entrepreneurs are happier than people who work a job for someone else. That's usually because they know themselves better because self-analysis is necessary to succeed. Money by itself is probably not enough of a reason to go on this journey, but I get that some people want the cash. Just don't fool yourself that money equals happiness.

DBAS: I'll take being happy over being rich but let's be greedy and get both.

How much is enough?

If you did answer money to the previous questions, the next question to ask yourself is how much is enough money? There are only so many cars you can drive, planes you can fly, and lobsters you can eat. There's the law of diminishing returns. Where the more you do something, the less rewarding it is.

If you are in it for the money, then you should have an actual number that you are shooting for when you start. Then ask yourself why you picked that number. If you plucked a number out of thin air it's likely ego. Put a little more thought into what you want that money to provide.

Success to create envy or self-confidence?

Another reason people start their own businesses is to prove themselves. People want to show the world who they are and what they're capable of. This is one that is harder to recognize in yourself before your journey. Be aware if you're trying to prove something to yourself or if you have a chip on your shoulder. That can be a bottomless pit that you're trying to prove yourself to your parents, your friends or whomever. Or it could be motivation. Truth is that it will likely be a mix of multiple things. (Spoiler alert)

You can't see a chip on your shoulder in the mirror.

I know that there were people in my life that I wanted to show I could follow through on my dreams. In the end, as success came in, there was a small bit of joy in having them see my accomplishments. Yet it felt shallow. That's when I switched over to feeling more self-satisfaction that I demonstrated I could do it to myself.

Reasons for starting your own business are kind of all over the map. If you're doing it to prove yourself, and that's on the top of your list, you're probably psychotic. Which may prove valuable in being an entrepreneur. LOL.

Having a chip on your shoulder isn't bad. This is all about knowing yourself. If you find this to be your motivation, then you must use it, you have to leverage it. When you have to dig deep on a tough day you can think about that person that mistreated you or said you couldn't do this. You say, "fuck you" to them in your mind. You say, "I'm going to power through this and work harder, endure more because I want to show that asshole that I can do this." Whatever floats your boat.

Freedom is just another word for nothing left to lose.

The next concept is probably the number one reason people should start a business. The goal of personal freedom. People want to be their own boss. I always say that's great. Yet remember, you have just enough rope to hang yourself. Meaning, you make your own laws, you make your own rules. You set the hours that the business is open. If you want to be open from noon to seven, sure, why not. You can tell everybody that your business is located in Hawaii yet it's actually in New York City and operating on a completely different time zone. It's your business you can do whatever you want with it for better or worse.

Freedom Ain't Free.

If freedom is your goal, it probably should be married with some of the other goals. Freedom itself is a wonderful thing, but in the wrong hands it doesn't work so well. Think of when you were a kid at school, the path is set in front of you. You must complete this class and your goal is to get a high grade, that easily followed path goes away when you leave school. There's certainly more of that in a corporate environment, in a job where you're working for somebody else. You're getting evaluated and looking for the approval of your boss. With the freedom of being an entrepreneur, you no longer have that goal set for you.

Freedom may be the best internal reason to start your own business. It doesn't mean you're going to be any more successful. Actually, wanting to prove people wrong and desiring money means you're probably more likely to succeed. This is because you're a deviant. Yet in the end, independence was probably the reason that you thought being your own boss was a good idea in the first place.

DBAS: At first, freedom and profit can seem like they go hand in hand. Yet, if the business gets too big you may lose that sense of freedom and become a slave to your own creation.

Job or Career Security- You're not Fired.

Another personal goal is that of job security. Job Security is a myth for 90% of professions. It is a thing of the past, working for one company for 40 years. If you work for somebody else, they can fire you whenever they want. I do love when people talk about job security and they say "oh if I if I start my own business, I wouldn't know if I was going to get a paycheck next week. I wouldn't know where the money is going to come from." Yet, you only have the illusion of security wherever you work right now.

You may have no idea what's going on in the front office of your place of employment, you may have no idea of what their goals are and you're at their whim. So, the security of being an entrepreneur is that your life is in your own hands. You're protected in knowing the fact that if you succeed you will be rewarded. However, there are no guarantees in life.

Eat What You Kill

A true entrepreneur wants to eat what you kill, meaning you don't want to do well and watch somebody else get the spoils of your hard labor. If you do well at work you want the reward, if you do poorly you'll take the consequences.

Variety of Tasks

The next reason that I would add would be variety. Having a life that is not monotonous. When you have your own business, you perform a lot of different tasks. Now you may go to work every day and do pretty much the same thing all day within a range, but you yearn for variety. You want to negotiate. You want to sell. You want to design a web site. You want to travel. You want to meet people. You want to learn new things. You want to have constantly new challenges and entrepreneurship will offer that.

It's a rare thing where you'll find this level of variety being an employee because usually your management will want to stick you in a box. Try to control your development and your tasks because it's much easier to manage.

Variety is the spice of life and another great reason to become an entrepreneur. You wake up every day and do a bunch of different things, so you're going to have a more fulfilled life.

Self-Actualization

Another area which is a little touchier would be self-actualization. A noble reason to start your own business. This is where you love the work so much and you love the ideas so much that you feel that the world must have it. There are many people over time that are so engrossed in their pursuit it just propels them. It's not about the money, it's not about the freedom, not about proving themselves. They want to see the idea/product come to life and the other benefits are just biproducts. That's all well and good, but you can't eat good vibes or pay the rent with inner peace. So, make sure there is some balance with revenue.

All Things in Moderation *Except Passion

Hopefully your goals are a balance of all these things. In a perfect world you want to love what you're going to do. If you're going to get into your own business, you should be passionate about it.

That's an important thing. You must have that passion but it probably is going to be hard to find something that fits exactly what you do. It doesn't have to be the products or service that you have passion for. It could be the method or technology used. As long as some part of the business gets your motor running you are ok.

Final Words: Think about your motivation. What are your goals in starting this business? Age does matter because depending on your age, your goals are going to be different.

Contemplate the different factors that can play into deciding the actual reasons for your business journey with where your life resides in reality. Whether it's money, improving yourself, freedom, self-actualization, security, or variety in task. Nothing should stop you from starting your own business if you are determined. Knowing why you are doing it will make it much easier to achieve success.

Chapter 5: Doing Everything and Mapping the Path

Wearing Many Hats

How many hats can you wear? When you become an entrepreneur, you're going to have to do a variety of different tasks. Some people are more comfortable with wearing a lot of hats than others. Jack of all trades master of none, maybe?

When you start a company, you must be willing to do any task to succeed. You may have to be a graphic designer, a programmer, a photographer, a lawyer, a writer, a negotiator or a janitor. All which I did in my first business.

Learning New Things: Do It Yourself and Save Money

I had to learn about a variety of topics for example signing contracts for hardware. I couldn't afford a lawyer and because anything you can do yourself saves money, I took the risk. This doesn't mean you have to do everything yourself. But you only have so much money and so much time. You need to find ways to stretch your dollar.

My first internet business was putting together travel guides. We didn't hire photographers because that would have been expensive. I knew how a camera worked so we just went to different places and took the pictures ourselves. You'd be amazed how quickly you learn. We shot at the Smithsonian and all through Washington D.C.. Myself and my business partner being amateur photographers, yet the results weren't that far from a professional photographer. (This was in the dark ages before camera phones).

Swiss Army Knife and Atom Bomb

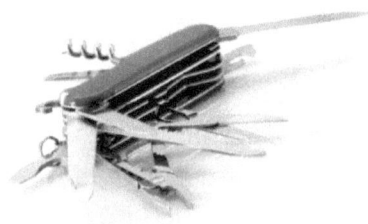 There really are no bounds to what you may have to learn to survive and succeed. You must be both a Swiss army knife and an atom bomb all at once. At the core of your business you must be exceptional at something, but you also need to be able to handle a bunch of different things. Like a Swiss army knife.

Next time you are in any business just look around and think about all the things that must come together for it to function. Lights, furniture, cleaning, accounting, cash in the register, inventory, work schedule, and so on.

Wearing many hats means you're probably going to have to learn things that have nothing to do with your business. Depending on your background; where you live, past jobs, there are certain tasks you never had to deal with.

Do you know how to snake a toilet? Or a plumber to call. The first time I had an office I hadn't encountered plumbing problems before. I learned fast. Who plows the snow in your parking lot? Do you know how to fix an internet router? Some of these things can be avoided by not having a physical location, but there is likely no maintenance department or human resources to help you out. You are the head of every department when you start.

Everybody thinks about the boardroom when they think of business knowledge. Can I negotiate well? Can I raise the capital? Proving your concept is a disruptor. But these nitty gritty details, keep the trains running on time. The ability to pivot to things that are so outside of your comfort zone is key to being a good entrepreneur.

In the world we live in it is easier to outsource a lot of the stuff. But guess what, being able to outsource is a skill that you may not have yet. Picking the right people to do a job even if you're paying somebody else to do it is important.

DBAS: You can't do everything yourself. Even if you could it's not a long-term strategy. Pick your battles carefully.

Being Decisive

You're going to be asked to make a lot of decisions as an entrepreneur. This is one of the more annoying parts. When you plunk yourself down to begin working, no one tells you what to do. In most past jobs you had to make decisions, but they were likely very specific to your role. When you're an entrepreneur you must decide everything. Do I need an office, or can I work from home? If you are getting an office, you are faced with more choices. How big of an office do I need? Who should I use for Wi-Fi? Should I get cable? Should I get this? Should I get that? Everything is going to be on you.

Who's your health insurance provider?

How much health insurance do you need?

What's the deductible you want?

A lot of these things are about being a grown up but as an entrepreneur nobody's going to help you make these decisions. Ever thought much about office furniture? Well, you will now. Some of this is fun the first time around. Oh, we're going to get our own desks. Which one are we going to pick out? (And by the way, don't spend a lot of money on office furniture. There are many ways to get used office furniture. Or portable stuff which is collapsible.)

What should you use for accounting, Freshbooks or Quickbooks? There are a million examples and you probably have thought of some. If you're not a person who is capable of making decisions quickly this may be an issue. Best thing is to know the difference between a large decision and a small decision. Some items are worth spending time deciding others can just be time sucks.

Final Words:

Starting your own business requires you to do a wide swath of functions. Be open to that.

Also, you must be decisive. That doesn't mean you should make snap decisions. You must be able to evaluate and see how much work and effort should go into each choice . Being able to make decisions effectively is just another part of being an entrepreneur.

Chapter 6: Are You a Solo Act or a Band?

Partners – Co-Founders: Two Heads May Be Better than One

Startups are usually an arduous adventure. Often having more than just yourself at the outset can have many benefits. So, should you have a co-founder? If more people came up with the concept than yourself, you're already there. Yet, if you are alone at the initially, you can ask the question "do I need a cofounder?"

Start simply with do you have someone in mind? To make your business work are you good at one part and they're good at another. You are an expert at tech and they're good at marketing. That's chocolate and peanut butter. However, sometimes there's overlap in skill sets and it's a less complimentary match. Just getting talented people at the core of the business can be enough. There are many benefits to having a cofounder.

BIG Founders – Big Fun

I remember when I was starting BIG Inc and I planned on partnering with my best friend from college. This topic came up in conversation with a businessman I knew up in New York. He was skeptical about partners and asked me why I was going to take this person on. "Why? Do you want somebody to eat lunch with? Because that seems ridiculous to me." (He was a bit of an asshole)

That comment stuck with me and that does sound silly on the surface. Sometimes at the outset of a business it's not clear who is good or not. So, teaming up with another person is less crystalized. For many years at the beginning of our business, one of the best parts of the day was when the small team would go out to lunch together. I would never have a partner just to lunch with, but don't underestimate the value of sharing the experience with somebody.

Me, I got lucky to have the pleasure of working with my best friend and co-founder Ron Gabriele for a decade. Going into the venture I didn't know what either of our responsibilities would be. Yet I knew he was smart, great with people, fun to be around and a solid balance to my personality. Over time each of us gravitated to part of the business that suited our skills. Sharing that journey with him was one of the most rewarding and enjoyable parts of my business career.

It's been proven that co-founders do better than solo founders of companies. That's an important thing to understand. A lot of it has to do with two heads being better than one. Having two different points of view has tremendous value.

I derived additional worth in having "an audience". What I mean by this is that I would go into my office and solve a problem out of thin air. Eureka moments. The ability to go to my co-founder and say "Oh my god look at this solution.

Imagine what this is going to mean for our future." This created an energetic back and forth by having somebody to share it with. Someone who would be equally as excited about your efforts.

This would also create emotional highs that I would seek again and again. Which helped propel me during difficult times. Seeking those exciting moments. You must know yourself, for me it was important to get applause when I've done something amazing. I know this isn't the best quality to have but being honest with yourself is easier than changing who you are. If you're by yourself there's nobody there to clap and that's it. Life is best shared.

Also, by having a cofounder you have someone who is counting on you to do your part. I often find that I have an easier time letting myself down than I do others. Having a partner creates accountability that you may lack without one.

DBAS: Having partners is about more than just increasing profit. There is a human element that shouldn't be ignored.

Han Solo is better than divorce

On the other side, going it alone is totally acceptable. Even in the example above I worked on the company for 6 months by myself before I thought it worth bringing someone else in. Timing and circumstances play a role as well. Locating a co-founder isn't as easy as one two three. (Although there are websites for this exact purpose these days.) When I was younger, I was around a lot of people who were in similar circumstances to myself, who could take risks. As you get older or as your circumstances are more particular, it's harder to find somebody who matches you. Cofounding is like a marriage of sorts. You don't want the wrong marriage. Don't get a co-founder just for the sake of it. And try to stick to the idea of people who aren't assholes.

When It's Right It's Right

You must have somebody who complements your skills to help you become successful. Exactly what that is, may be as simple as ABC. I can do A and B and they can do C and D. However, there's usually more to it. There are personalities that get involved and you must question yourself about how this will work 2, 5, 20 years from now. Have you ever worked with this person in any way, shape or form? You should stress test the partnership if you haven't worked together before. Find something that might be a little bit complicated like having them help you move, build furniture, or go on a road trip. Something where tensions will probably get high and see how it goes.

Cofounders are in the foxhole with you. They have to have your back and you have theirs. Just know what you are getting into and your reasons for doing so. It's better to find out sooner rather than later, if you are a good match.

Final Words: Go it alone or start your company with others, both are solid paths. Know who you are and what works best for you. If you do work with others, make sure that they are the right match or it can be a death blow.

Chapter 7: Wit, Grit, and Bullshit

In the world of entrepreneurship your role models are not going to always be the most upstanding people. Some may be very flawed human beings. A person who I emulated to an extent was a gentleman by the name of Don King. Don was a very famous boxing promoter and a quote machine. One of my favorites is:

> *"Man I've been to jail. It was hell in there. But I survived. They put me back. I'll come out again. I'm one of the world's greatest survivors. I'll always survive because I've got the right combination of wit, grit and bullshit"*

 If you know Don King and know his speech pattern, I'm probably not doing it justice but damn that man could speak. He could turn any sentence into gold. I've always felt like those three things are what make up a great entrepreneur. Wit, Grit, and Bullshit. Let's examine each of them for a second.

Wit: The Right Kind of Smarts

The first thing is wit. Are you smart and quick? I'm asking you questions to try to figure out what you think of yourself. Are you intelligent? Do other people think you're smart? Being smart is one part of wit, the other is being snappy with its use.

A benefit of intellect is being able to look at a situation quickly and come up with a strategic plan. If you have a level of intelligence that exceeds others it will give you an advantage. We aren't talking about book smart. I'm not telling you that you must have a 180 IQ. Sometimes intellect of that magnitude stands in your way. Yet if you're dull, starting your own business can be overwhelming. I'm not trying to talk you out of it, but the wiser you are, the better off you're going to be.

Experience Equals Intelligence

Experience can be a decent supplement for wit. Have you ever worked in this field before? Using your intellect to have an advantage over the competition is the goal. If your knowledge is partially comprised of experience, keep that in mind as you choose your business. Say you are a math whiz but you want to open your own candy shop. One really has nothing to do with the other. Just make sure that you know where your skills apply to this business. If you've worked in the business previously , then you're more likely to see your wits in action.

If you're in a trade and you're excellent at it, that doesn't mean you can run your own business. You could be an amazing plumber, accountant or a rocket scientist just because you're adept doesn't mean you can be an entrepreneur. Wit is the way you use your knowledge to solve problems or work with others. Wit is just one element that you need. There's far more to being a successful entrepreneur than just being smart.

Grit: Survive and Advance

Grit is about how you're going to perform in the face of adversity. How you're going to deal with the grind of being an entrepreneur. Are you willing to put in long hours without guarantee of rewards? Are you willing to destroy whatever routine you might have in your life?

The path of an entrepreneur is fraught with peril. There is no direct route because things are going to change every day. This is an amazing benefit that your life will be interesting, but it is much more difficult especially at the outset. Grit will help you stick to a plan when the road looks hard. Give me the type of person who can roll with the punches and keep pushing forward. That person has grit and it's a massive part of what you need to succeed on your own.

In Over Your Head

A way to measure your grit would be to think of a time in your life where you were in over your head. And how did it go? Did it scar you? Did it change your life? If you haven't had that happen to you yet, where you felt completely in overwhelmed that's not a bad thing. You have led a charmed life. That will change if you start your own business. LOL.

Grit is pure determination. Something inside that doesn't let you stop. Remember a moment tin where you refused to turn back or take no for an answer. Is that something you are comfortable with? Is it a something you'd welcome again?

Often, I find that most things in life that are worthwhile I wouldn't have taken on if I knew how hard they were beforehand. I just tossed my cap over the wall and had no choice but to figure out how to get to the other side. That is the grit, I saw these things through once I was in the fight.

Recently, a friend of mine told me "You are indestructible". This was an interesting thing to say to someone and I thought on it for a while. No one is completely bulletproof, but on some level, yes, I am indestructible, and you are too. You can try to set us on fire, try to blow us up, try nine million different ways to destroy us and we'll just walk through them.

I do this because I don't know any other way, I only know how to go forward. That's part of what has shepherded me through business my whole life. It sounds like you need to be The Terminator to be an entrepreneur. You don't, but it sure would help.

Grit is needed to succeed in the long term. Luck can help you out at times. But grit will see you through when your luck isn't so great.

When Amex Tried to Kill Me

One event that I am reminded of by this topic is when I was in way over my head with ReserveVacations.com. A business where I raised a large sum of capital. Taking on more money than I needed, and it ended up growing faster than it should have.

The business model was where vacation ownership companies were subsidizing people's travel to get them to hear their presentation. People would pay say $499 for a trip that actually cost $799. We would cover the difference and eventually get $500 from the vacation ownership company.   Our typical sale was about 90 days before the trip and wouldn't get paid by the vacation ownership companies till 60-90 days after the person travelled.

Maybe Leave Home Without It

Part of how we operated was using our corporate American Express card to pay expenses including hotel inventory. This gave us an extra 30 days of cash flow because of the billing cycle and as a bonus we earned American Express rewards points. One day out of the blue, American Express calls and says we're pulling your line of credit. We had never missed a payment, we often paid ahead of time. Our bills were hundreds of thousands of dollars and suddenly they wanted to be paid right away.

The issue was we were now counting on this cash flow to spend money on advertising to bring in sales to pay the bill. We were owed significant money from vendors, but that wouldn't come in for months. Hence, we had a large hole that we needed to fill immediately.

I didn't know how we were going to able to pay them so quickly. A partner of mine had personally signed for this credit card. I didn't want this bill to have negative ramifications on him. Obviously counting on this line of credit and signing it up in his name were mistakes, but at this point that is hindsight. This threw me upside down. Our business was brought to a complete halt. I was in way over my head and if we didn't find solutions to get cash and keep the business moving, we were dead and buried.

Pressure is What Makes Diamonds.

The only thing I could do was get smarter and create a better business. As the walls were crumbling, we figured out how to create more cash flow in a short period of time. This could help cover the shortfall. We fixed this by examining our model and looking for sales that weren't cash flow negative.(Duh) A lot of the packages we sold required hotel rooms which we had to pay for up front (cash flow negative). We also sold others that centered on park tickets (like Disney World). These we didn't have to pay for till the time the person travelled, making them cash flow positive.

Thinking about it now and writing about it, the business seems all neat and tidy. The situation was nothing like that at the time. This was my nightmare. Flipping the model and finding fresh money seems elementary now, but I wasn't handed the answers. I could have run for the hills and let other people hold the bag. None of the debt was in my name and I could have folded but I didn't. I just fought and fought. The changes I made didn't completely save us. I bought us some time. GRIT.

This was only part of the solution; I fixed the model, but I needed to simultaneously pay AMEX and have money to spend on advertising. A cash infusion would go a long way to bridging the gap.

DBAS: Tough times make tough people. Dig in and you will find the answers.

Cartels are Not for Kids

Around this time, we had been in discussions with a big operator in Mexico about doing a partnership on a new product we had in development. Off to Cancun I went to work out a deal to get us some much needed cash. This Mexican company was going to bulk purchase licenses for our new travel club software. Discussions advanced quickly. I cut the bullshit and told them that I wanted X dollars for Y products. I demoed the software for 30 of their top brass and executives. They loved the product and agreed. Hooray, right?

Turns out these guys were not really on the up and up. They were timeshare operators and their core was about using every sales tactic in the book to get the best result for them. These master manipulators figured out a way to hold me "hostage" in Mexico for 96 hours. I wasn't physically held hostage. It was a prison of the mind. One of my hopes and dreams. They would say "we're going to sign the deal in the morning" and have me postpone my flight home. Then put me up at one of their 5 star resorts and take me out on the town. Treating me like the crown price of Zumunda. (What a schmuck I was)

This pattern of delay and pushbacks went on for 3 days in a row. At the outset I was so relieved that I was going to get the deal I needed that I didn't think twice. All I could ponder is that I had to have this deal because I wasn't going to let my partner get stuck with all of the debt from AMEX. The cash would also allow us to push our new model and get the ship right. I was up against it and let my guard down during this process. I slipped and let them know my situation. My thought was if I was honest with them about my needs for cash that it would cut through the bullshit. They wanted and loved my product and I was asking a fair price. Yet they couldn't fight their nature. They began twisting the screws and kept moving the goalposts. I started to sense something wasn't right.

DBAS: Avoid revealing too much information about your position in negotiations. Seasoned pros will use any tidbit they have against you.

Finally, push came to shove and I couldn't take it anymore. I was under pressure like I had never felt before to get this deal done. They came to me with a new updated offer which would have kept me a float for a few months, but it was straight robbery. I had revealed that I was vulnerable. They chose to try and fuck me instead of taking a agreement that was already wonderful for them. What choice did I have, I needed the money? So, I did what I thought was the right thing. I told them to **go fuck themselves. GRIT.**

Escape from Cancun

That's right, even with my back up to the wall, in a foreign country, I wasn't going to curl up and die. A funny side note, I finally had had enough and went back to my hotel to pack. When I got into the room, I was so frustrated I flung an ashtray off a table. I didn't realize that the tabletop was not connected to the base, so the tabletop tumbled across the room. The top was made of marble tile and cracked when it hit the ground. Full of emotion I picked up my shit and got out of Dodge.

As I am at the airport waiting for my flight, I get a call from the CEO of the Mexican Timeshare company saying I trashed my room and they wanted me to pay thousands in damage. All I did was push an ashtray off of a table and yes, I was trying to break a very small thing but it turned into a larger thing. These guys made it out like I went Keith Richards on the room. They even tried to charge the credit card I left at the desk, but I didn't have enough spending power for the charge to go through. But I was finally able to see through this as just another attempt to get me to take their deal. I had the wit and grit I needed to again tell them to fuck off. I flew back to the states and during the 3-hour flight I outlined a plan to rally the troops and solve the problem without these fuckers.

You're going to get in over your head and it's going to feel like you're drowning. Desperately grasping for anything to hold on to get a grip. That's where you need that grit. Hopefully, there will be people that have your back like my partners in this story. Yet when you're trapped in your version of a resort in Cancun Mexico, being manipulated by masters, you feel all alone. Likely, you're going to be tested in ways you've never considered. Dig in. Grit. Have the gumption to stand up to whatever challenges hit you. Grit can make you indestructible and able to walk through the fire.

Bullshit In and Out

You got the wit and the grit. Now, do you have the bullshit? Bullshit is broken into two parts. Can you create bullshit and can you detect bullshit?

Being a bullshitter I ask, how well can you think on your feet? How good are you at getting people to believe the bright side of a story? My inner bullshitter came to me early. When I was in high school, I competed in mock trial competitions. One year, I was a prosecutor, another I was a witness. The whole idea of it was to prove that you can think on your feet. Opponents would try to maneuver you and paint you into a corner with their questions. Not only did you have to come up with the right answer, you had to make it sound believable. This came naturally to me and I ended up undefeated in a mock trial. My wit could see their traps coming. Then my BS found a response to thwart their plans in a way that the judge and jury found believable.

Some would ask what's the difference between wit and bullshit? They are interlinked on some levels. Bullshit is about having the wit you need to come up with an answer, but also about having the ability to spin a yarn that is convincing , even though it's not the whole story. With wit you can put it down on paper and take time to get the answer, but bullshit just flows from within on the spot. Being able to get someone to believe your message is far more than the words that come out of your mouth. Bullshitting requires you to be a storyteller. You're taking someone on a journey of where you want them to go.

> ### Being full of shit and being a bullshitter are different things
>
> One thing that separates entrepreneurs from the average person is they actually do things. In general people are 99 percent full of shit. Entrepreneurs are only 95 percent full of shit. That 4 percent makes all the difference in the world. Simply because we do four times as much of what we talk about. My point is that everybody's full of crap. Entrepreneurs are just a little less full of crap.

Have You Bullshitted Today?

We talked about having gambled before and the willingness to take a risk. Some people are squeamish with risk and bullshit also makes a lot of people uncomfortable. Some call it salesmanship but let us be frank. Its bullshitting.

BRAIN TRAINING

Brain Exercise:
A good test for this is to go out into the world and make your case to a stranger about the idea for your business. Go somewhere in public, a bar, gym, or restaurant. Wherever you feel comfortable. Strike up a conversation with a total stranger. Then I want you to project upon them not where your business is now, but where your business is going to be in six months. Act as if

you were at that advanced stage right now. You're going to pretend as if things have happened exactly as you hoped. Of course, it won't happen that way but you're going to pretend for the sake of this exercise. Try not to do too much rehearsal of answers and invite questions from the person with whom you are speaking. This is an excellent measure of your bullshitting prowess.

You must have met people who do this in real life. We encounter bullshitters all the time. People who exaggerate the truth or run away with the circus with their stories. Where something a little exciting is happening in their life and they've blown it up to make it seem thrilling. A simple example someone gets a job interview for an entry level position. Then they make it out like they are going to be running the company. If they do it convincingly, they are a good bullshitter.

Bullshitting helps you have the ability to project confidence for the future and your vision of the company. At some point you're going to have to sell yourself, whether it be to investors to raise capital or to sell to potential clients of your product. Make them dream along with you and get them to buy into it. You're capable of spinning bullshit, go out there and try. See how you do because it will become handy.

Side Tracked: Using Your BS Powers

Corporate Narrative

You're going to have to create your company's "story" if you're raising funds or when you're building your company. To position your business in the market the way you want, you create an engaging story. People want to think that they're logical number crunchers and it's all about the best product or best price when in fact they are attracted to a good story just as much. People like a tale they can easily retell and make others excited.

Use archetypes like the whiz kid, the underdog, or the comeback. You must figure out the details of your story for your business. Who's the villain and who's the hero? Then try to find a way to push that out into the world. Be it through your own blog on your or social media which is great for fostering narratives.

You can create the folklore you want people to think about your product or your service on your own. (Think of Apple starting in a garage. Does that really matter? No, but it makes a great story) Be the champion of your own narrative, never let others hijack it.

Eventually your story will be set in stone, whether you like it or not. But as you're starting it you can have an opportunity to create stories or plant stories. I'm not talking about doing something unethical. If you don't create the story or tell the story about how you're the hero and who the villain is you're going to force other people to try to figure it out. Why not just lay it out there? That you're the people who figured out how to look inside the box and come out with magic. How nobody else had ever done what you have and that's why it's so wonderful. Craft your narrative as it will make everything easier if you have a good story to tell.

How's Your Bullshit Detector?

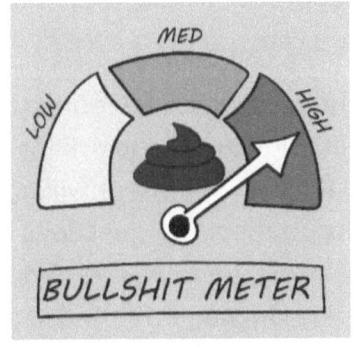

Now Don King didn't say anything about sensing bullshit, but if you're going to talk about bullshit in business it is a two-way street. You've got to be able to BS but you've also got to be able to see it coming. You've got to have a bullshit detector.

There's no doubt that people in business will try to bullshit you. Try to tell you that the world they're bringing you into is an amazing place. That you need them to get where you want to go. They can come in many forms, they don't always look like a used car salesman or come from a rinky-dink company. They are anybody who's trying to get you to part with assets (time, money or information). Salespeople are usually the most harmless and easy to spot. As an entrepreneur you should be getting into strategic partnerships, investments, contracts and affiliate deals. All sorts of situations where you're going to count on somebody else's ability to perform to have success yourself.

You must be able to sniff out whether the person on the other end of your deal is full of shit. If not, you could be running 100 miles per hour into a brick wall. All too often people hear what they want to hear. Avoid this as best as you can.

The best ways I've found to detect BS is to hammer people with questions and ask for evidence to back up their claims. If they are unwilling to commit to hard numbers or they deflect the questions those are red flags. The verbal answers are only part of detecting the BS. Look at their body language. Try and see what makes them uncomfortable. Good people are usually squeamish when you ask them to do shady things. Poke and prod. It's worth the extra few minutes to get a more complete picture.

DBAS: Bullshit is everywhere. Most of it is harmless. Knowing the difference between the important and the innocuous is the key.

Beware of False Prophets

We All Get Fooled Sometimes: Yes, I've been a schmuck plenty.

My bullshit detector wasn't always working properly. I remember during the IPO process for Hotels.com I got duped good. There was a guy who worked for Hotels.com and he convinced the major investment banks that he was the cornerstone of their affiliate division. At the time we were the largest Hotels.com affiliate making up 5% of their total business. This guy made me feel like he had my back by telling me inside gossip on the company. This made me loyal to him as he seemed to have my best interest at heart. Not only was I loyal to him against my own benefit but I trusted what he was saying as if it came from god himself. All because he gave me some inside info that made me feel important. A lot of what he had told me were outright lies, but for some reason I believed him. Probably because they played to my ego.

I have since met other colleagues in my industry who ended up with the same problem with this guy. He was amazing at selling the story of how important he was to his company. How he inserted himself in the exact right place to control distribution of hotel sales. The truth was he wasn't much of anything other than good at spinning a yarn. Did that cost me in the end? Yes, in a couple of ways.

In the Hotels.com IPO, where we got friends and family stock, we probably would have gotten a lot more if I had known this guy was a liar. He told me how hard I could push and what other people were getting. So when we got our allotment, I thought we had done well. Turns out we probably could have received at least double

Right after the IPO, this person jumped ship to a smaller competitor. He tried to get us to leave our current deal as the largest reseller for Hotels.com. We got all the way down the road to where we almost shifted all our sites and distribution. This would have been a massive undertaking. Fortunately for us the story took a weird turn. Coincidentally he visited Atlantic City and called us to pick him up unexpectedly. He said he was dodging the police. (WTF) He claimed that he was urinating in public and the cops saw him. We rushed to pick him up, but he had taken bullshit too far. He was telling us a tale about how things went down and knowing the city like the back of my hand I knew he was fibbing. This incident didn't matter much on the surface, but after that I started asking questions of people. Ones he told me never to talk to because they were "against me". His whole house of cards fell and he was out of his job in a month. (Dumb Luck)

He bullshitted me good. He knew my soft spots and played to them. You're going to live and learn. Don't be seduced by the bullshit. Be able to root it out and know how to spin it yourself. The old saying it takes one to know one.

DBAS: Everyone is a schmuck sometime. Don't beat yourself up too bad. Just learn from it best you can.

Final Words:

Wit, Grit and Bullshit is a nice sounding phrase to encapsulate what it takes to be an entrepreneur. You need to be quick on your feet and be able to take a punch. Determination and skill with a little fertilizer will get you a long way to becoming a successful entrepreneur.

Chapter 8: Ideas

Moving on to the next phase of the conversation. You've decided that going into business for yourself, and being an entrepreneur is what you want. Now we're going to look at your idea. I spend a decent amount of time reviewing businesses at various stages of development. At first glance you don't look at much more than their basic concept. Things like team quality and capitalization are less important in that first impression phase. This is important to assessing your idea, as it will likely be apparent to a seasoned entrepreneur whether you have a chance at success purely based on your concept. But there are some exceptions.

Being Right 90% of the Time and Big Misses

Through my research and reading, I see about 10 new companies every week. 9 out of 10 of them look like they are going to fail. Truth be told, I'm almost always right about the one that I think will succeed. Of the other nine that I predict are going to fail, one of them usually succeeds. That's a pretty good track record of being able to assess a good company or a bad company. Yet amongst those nine that I say are going to fail, the one that succeeds often is a huge business. These are often much harder to envision success because of the need for disruption. The market conditions and status quo will need to be altered in a way that at the moment does not seem logical.

For some reason it's much easier to remember the big businesses that I was wrong about than the ones I was correct. Off the top of my head Twitter, Facebook, Uber and Airbnb were companies I thought were all going to fail. When I initially heard of Friendster and Facebook, the idea of having friends on the Internet seemed like the dumbest thing in the world. This was in the early 2000s and the closest thing to a functioning social network was classmates.com. Which was a way to find people from your high school.

I may just have a blind spot for social media. Twitter seemed just like an app made up of Facebook status. Why would anyone want a microblogging platform? Turns out a lot of people did.

Both businesses were harder to envision because they required a high level of critical mass to be a success. Meaning without a large user base, they would fail. There is no clear path to getting the large adoption rate. It feels to me like catching lightning in a bottle.

Another two concepts that were hard to see succeeding were Airbnb and Uber. The reason for missing these was they ran against conventional law. Both of those companies skirted previous law and entrenched industries. Uber dodged the taxi laws and Airbnb circumvented vacation rental law or condo association red tape.

Both concepts also benefited from perfect timing. The economy crashed in 2008 and people relaxed their hold on old laws and looked for any method of driving revenue. Additionally, just like the social network companies Uber and Airbnb required critical mass to work. Without enough buyers and sellers the marketplace couldn't grow. The great recession created a pool of tons of drivers for Uber and excess real estate inventory for Airbnb. Out of chaos comes great opportunity. It is often easier to create these disruptors during downswings than robust economic conditions.

Some ideas may seem bad by conventional measure, but they can be good. Not everybody can see that, even a trained eye like myself. Not everybody can have the vision. This is not the norm.

Which category would your idea fall? Would it be the one out of ten which can't miss? Or the one of nine which looks like it's going to miss but turns into something big.

Does your business require critical mass?

I mentioned this factor earlier and it's worth looking at a bit closer. When you're examining your idea, you must ask what is it going to take to succeed. If it's a critical mass business, which requires you to build a network, these are tricky to forecast their success. Usually they are all or nothing. If there's nobody on Facebook it doesn't work. All networks operate that way. They need enough people using the product to make it worthwhile for others to use it.

A few other examples are gambling sites like Draft Kings or Pokerstars. Both enormous billion-dollar businesses that were able to capture critical mass. If you don't have enough people playing, it doesn't work out. People need others to play against. These systems also feed off themselves. They usually grow geometrically because new users make the games more attractive.

Marketplaces like a Craigslist, eBay or Etsy are also critical mass businesses. If there aren't enough buyers, there won't be enough sellers. No one wants to put in the effort to sell products on a marketplace if no one is going to buy them. And conversely buyers don't like to shop in a place that has too few offerings.

Dating sites like Match or Tinder fall in this category. Review sites like Angies list or Yelp also need critical mass to succeed. Grubhub, Doordash, Uber Eats also have critical mass issues.

DBAS: Just because you have a good product doesn't mean you will immediately find critical mass. Lightning in a bottle is a bit of luck.

How you grow both sides of supply and demand can be magic. Best case scenario is that early adopters and word of mouth push the growth organically. However, many companies have been known to put their finger on the scale. They either bribe people to use their network or create fake entries. With billions of dollars at stake I can't really blame people for looking for creative ways to address this problem.

Once a company hits the critical mass tipping point it really takes off. This type of businesses is much harder to get off the ground but once they get going they take on a mind of their own. Self-perpetuating growth is a wonderful thing. Does your idea require many users to be successful? That doesn't make it better or worse it just makes the path different. The initial cost is going to be more expensive and profitability will likely take longer. You want to have a vision of your idea and how the success will come about. Don't take user adoption as a given because people who do that end up in a train wreck.

Is your idea unique? Does that matter?

Another question about your idea is has anybody else ever done this before. Usually the answer is yes, if you think that you've come up with a novel idea that nobody's tried or done before kudos to you. Yet, just because you are not aware of the existence of anybody doing what you plan doesn't mean there isn't anyone. Try using google to search for products or ideas like yours. I have often found that there are things similar to my concept, but not identical. Also, I will find that there are people working on a project like mine, but in a faraway part of the world which might not impact my development at all.

Don't fret if you find someone is already working on the same concept. (Assuming they don't have a patent that would block your entry.) Rarely does the company that invents something reap its greatest benefit. Friendster existed before Facebook. Facebook made all the money. Yahoo existed before Google. Google made all the money. I can't tell you how many food and grocery delivery companies preceded Postmates and Instacart. Don't just give up because someone else is in the game.

Usually it takes somebody to plant the flag and create the marketplace. Then somebody else comes along and learns how to make the profit. It's not bad if other people have done something similar before because they may have softened the ground for you. They will have uncovered a lot of the problems and errors in the market. Then you can learn from that. But it's important to see if anybody has had the same idea as you and how they have fared. Where did they go wrong if it isn't working or didn't work?

This is not a universal truth, obviously there will be times that you have an idea and someone is already doing it. You examine them and realize that the road would be too difficult based on how well they are executing their vision and the size of the market. Better to know now then find this out after you invest your life savings.

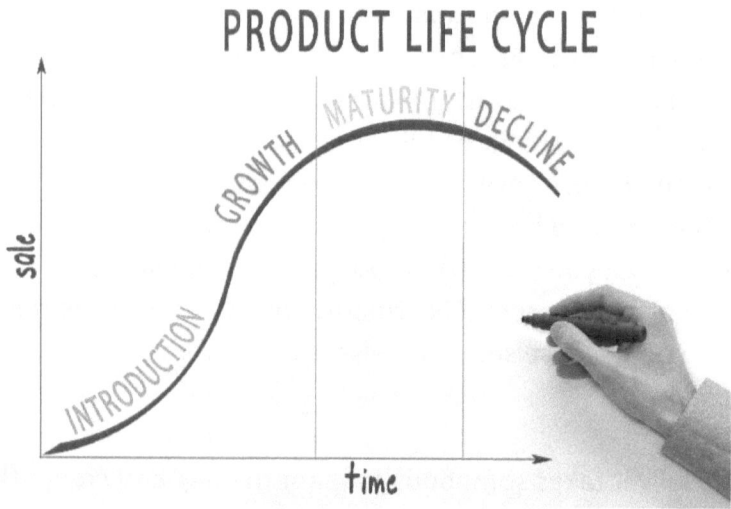

Business Life Cycle Factor

The next question to tackle is "what is the lifecycle of the business?" This is something people don't want to think about at the beginning of a company, but should. Lifecycle refers to how long this industry is going to last. Certain businesses need to be reinvented much more frequently than others. Wrangler Jeans is a business that's been around for a 100 years plus. It doesn't necessarily need to be reinvented every six months. Sure, there are some fashion changes, but the core business remains unchanged. Whereas something like Internet Security, the industry is changing every minute of every day. What is top of the line or cutting edge today may be useless in six months.

When you examine your idea knowing the projected lifestyle is important because you need to know your time horizon for being successful. If you think it's a good idea and it's going to take two or three years. Ask yourself where will this industry be by then? Will the market be about the same or much different than today? Predicting the future is obviously not a science but doing this simple thought experiment can save you a lot of grief down the road.

Business lifecycles always remind me of a movie with Danny Devito called Other People's Money. In it he plays a corporate raider nicknamed Larry the Liquidator. Who is in a hostile takeover of a manufacturing company. His character gives a great speech in which he addresses the shareholders about how and why he wants to break up this corporation. He takes the stage right after the long time C.E.O. makes an impassioned plea to save his company from Devito.

"You know, at one time, there must've been dozens of companies making buggy whips. And I'll bet the last company around was the one that made the best god-damn buggy whip you ever saw. Now how would you have liked to have been a stockholder in that company?"

Other People's Money (1991)

There are 5 parts of the business lifecycle; launch, growth, shakeout, maturity and decline. Nobody knows ahead of time how long each of these will last, but giving it some forethought should be a part of examining the value of your ideas. Don't be the best buggy whip maker around.

Are you surfing the wave or creating it?

Now that you know about business lifecycles and you can determine where your idea fits on the curve you can assess the health of the marketplace you plan to enter. Whether it will be affected by emerging technologies or is it a steady moving established sector. One thing I think you should keep in mind, is your idea part of a trendy industry which everybody is getting into because of a perceived "gold rush"? Cloud computing, big data, AI, Autonomous Vehicles, virtual reality, crypto currency... whatever is the flavor of the week.

Emerging Industries

Emerging industries are areas coming down the pike that are going to change the way the world works. Even if it's not your exact industry, new tech or products may tangentially change how things function . For example, autonomous cars are going to alter the world. Probably not quite as much as the internet did at the turn of the century, but it will be of that magnitude. This will impact almost every business as it will make the world smaller and more efficient. From food delivery to hotels to real estate. Just to name a few.

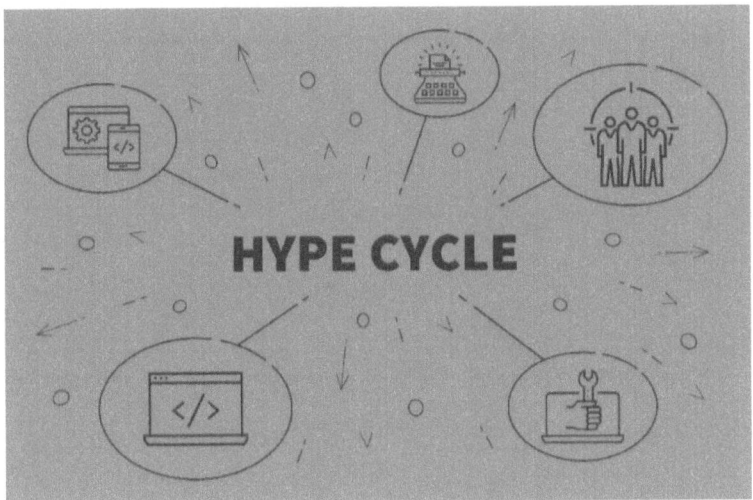

Virtual reality is going to impact entertainment and people's desire to leave their house. Drones will impact the way we deliver things. The availability of things that you couldn't have gotten readily yesterday will be available tomorrow. Say you're a chef who wants to open a restaurant in a city in the future you're going to be able to deliver your meals 100 miles outside your area using autonomous vehicles and drones. That's good for the top-quality restaurants, but this is going to hurt the local lower quality places. Now they are going to be competing with 100s or 1,000s of restaurants that previously couldn't service their customers.

3-D printing, The Internet of Things and many more concepts have the possibility of upending how business is transacted today. Some are real and some are science fiction mixed with hype. It is easy to get seduced into a brave new world. Just do it with open eyes.

When everyone is looking for gold, its a good time to be in the pick and shovel business

- Mark Twain

Picks and Shovels

If it's a trendy industry you want to be involved in, consider the picks and shovels philosophy. It is less risky to take advantage of a hot industry by selling the tools that businesses need to operate. Picks and shovels is a reference to the gold rush in Californian in the mid 1800's. Some people got rich from gold, but most didn't. The guys who sold the picks and shovels made a profit either way.

DBAS: Don't get sucked into a trend because of the hype. Timing is everything in an emerging industry.

Workshop Your Idea

How do you give your idea validity? Start simple, talk to other people about it. Run it by friends and family. If you're afraid of talking to people about your idea, then it may not be such a good one. Don't be afraid of people saying bad things, if you can't take somebody poking holes you're not going to get very far. Don't be so sensitive. Matter of fact, people taking shots at your brainchild should help test to see if you have the answers. If their criticism is on target it should send you back to the drawing board.

It is very hard to proofread your own work. People are often blind to problems in their own concepts. They will reread something over and over and never see a blatant mistake. This is because their mind won't let them see their own error. Road testing your idea will help uncover your blind spots and allow you to see what the path forward looks like more clearly.

Final Words: The idea is the ACORN that becomes the mighty oak. Do everything you can to understand it better. Look at it in the world of tomorrow as well as the world of today. Run it by people you trust.

Knowing where your idea fits in the landscape is important to being able to determine the path to success. Some ideas are unique while others have been tried before. Neither is better than the other. Just make sure you look at your idea from all angles before pushing forward.

Chapter 9: Business Plans. Overrated Yet Necessary

Creating a business plan is at its core a good idea. Fleshing out your concept into an executable plan is a necessity. They allow you to examine the path of your company, explain its goals, review the industry, research competitors and look at the numbers. Some people go overboard, but that doesn't have to be you. Finding a format that suits your style shouldn't be that hard.

My introduction into the need for a business plan came early in my career. When I was 19, audio books were a just coming into the mainstream. I was in college at the time and I had the "revolutionary" idea to take textbooks college and turn them into audio books. College students were always looking for shortcuts to get their work done faster and easier. In the 1990's this was a novel concept and I ran it by a few friends and family. All the people I spoke with gave me nothing but positive feedback. So, it was time to take the next step.

Through some connections I had made, I went to visit a lawyer. This was someone who not only understood intellectual property rights, but also was an entrepreneur himself.

He was a mountain of a man, probably 6 foot 6 and over 300 lbs. An intimidating figure, but he listened intently as I walked through the concept. After hearing my pitch, he says "I love the idea. OK let me see the plan."

I replied, "I just told you the plan." He went nuts on me, totally berserk. Again, this guy was enormous and not that I felt physically threatened, but just him moving around made for chaos. After catching his breath he says "You have nothing. Just an idea. Every asshole on the street has an idea. Put it down on paper. Make a plan."

I was kind of flabbergasted. Coming in I thought, I had this great idea that everyone I spoke to said can make a lot of money. What is this guy talking about that "I have nothing"? It took me a few minutes to regain my composure but then I began to realize what he meant. By committing your idea to paper you then allow other people to go through it without your narrative. Let them examine all the different parts. There is now a working document that enables the idea to grow and change as new information comes in. Without a plan you really don't have much, you're a just someone on a barstool talking shit.

Road Maps for Your Ideas

Ideas are important. Don't let my story give you the wrong impression. The idea is the acorn that becomes the mighty oak. Yet transitioning from an idea in your head to putting something on a piece of paper is a big step in the journey. People often get anxious about putting a business plan together. Thinking that the first version must be perfect. Don't be intimidated because the business plan, first and foremost is for you. It's not for investors or employees, that that'll happen down the road. The plan initially is for you to understand what it is you're trying to accomplish.

Here are a few simple questions your plan should answer:

- What is your product?
- How will you sell it?
- How much will it cost to make?
- What will you need to get started?
- Who are you competing against?
- Who will be on your team?
- Why are you best suited to make this happen?

You don't need to take too long to start. The first version is not a thesis. The truth is business plans don't survive the first contact. Meaning that your business plan is important to lay out the road map. Yet, something will occur to force you to alter your strategy. You must be able to adapt and overcome. The first place to show this is by making your business plan a living breathing document. One that allows for the ever-changing world to be weaved in a way that doesn't alter your core philosophy but incorporates necessary alterations.

"A good plan today is better than a
great plan tomorrow. "

Product

When you're putting together a business plan there's no true one way to do it. Often it has a lot to do with what business you're going to get into. I like to start by examining the product. What are your selling?

It doesn't matter whether it's a service or an actual physical product. Breakdown the details of what makes your product work. What makes it unique? Find a way to boil it down to a few sentence summary. Creating a list of features is a simple way to do this. You can get as detailed as you like, but always try to keep it organized. You want others to be able to follow your logic.

In the back of my mind I use a simple way of displaying what elements my product has and what other competing products don't. You have seen many graphics like this on websites. This may help in working up your feature list:

MINIMAL FREE	BASIC 9$/mo	ADVANCED 19$/mo	PRO 29$/mo
1	3	7	Unlimited
✓	✓	✓	✓
✗	✓	✓	✓
✗	✗	✓	✓
✗	✗	✗	✓

Marketing Sales: Get it to the people.

Next look at the marketing, sales and distribution. The type of product will dictate some of these answers.

- How are you going to get your product out there for people to buy?
- How are you going to advertise? On TV, Google, social media?
- Do you plan on using word of mouth?
- Do you intend on having an in-house sales force?
- What is the method of sale for your product?
- Is it physical retail or online?
- Is it to consumers or is it meant strictly for business?

While you are crafting the list of marketing methods be sure to explain why these are the right ones for your product. It is easy to say that you are going to run a massive TV brand building campaign. Yet it's more important to state what the expected outcome will be and why this is superior to other options. You can research the cost and impact of various sales and marketing methods. This is also an opportunity for you to show your experience and expertise if you have some in this field.

Industry and Studying the Competition

Do some poking around to find how big the industry is that you are entering. This matters because the overall size of the pie that exists relates to how much you need to get to be successful. Don't fool yourself though, just because an industry is large doesn't mean that it automatically makes it easier than a smaller one. Growth of an industry may prove to be more important than its size. I'd rather be in a space that is $10 billion total and growing at 20% a year than a 100$ billion space that is flat. None of this info is meant to disqualify your idea, but for you to be more certain about your ability to execute.

When you started researching your idea you should have found who else is servicing the same clientele as you plan to. They don't have to be the exact same. If you're starting an online blog about the San Diego food scene your competitors are potentially traditional media along with other bloggers. A competitor doesn't just mean the person that does the same thing as you, but the people you're competing with for the same dollars.

The more you know about your competitors the easier it is to pick out what they do well, and what they do poorly. Create a list of the competitors with a few bullet points that highlight their strengths and weaknesses. This helps in forming the product and marketing plans.

Also consider barriers to entry in this section. Are there things that keep anyone from off the street jumping into the market? A simple example would be a liquor license for a bar or liquor store. These are expensive and require approvals. Having one gives you a leg up on some random looking to compete with you.

DBAS: Be extensive with your search of competitors. Just because you haven't seen something before doesn't mean it's not out there in the universe somewhere.

STRATEGIC PARTNERSHIP

Strategic Partnerships: It's Who You Know

Strategic partnerships are a valuable part of a business plan. This is about what other companies you will be working with. These are relationships that will make executing your plan easier than going it alone. Sometimes you have no strategic partnerships going into a business, but obviously it would be better if you did. Don't let the fancy name fool you. These can come in the form of a good supplier. If you know someone who works at a store that will get you a bulk discount on purchase, that's a strategic relationship.

Let's look quickly at the example of when I was launching a new travel club. We were going to sell memberships for $10 a month. For this, members would get 40 percent off hotel rooms and other travel perks.

We had a strategic partnership in place with an online travel agency. This company had a million people a day visiting their travel web sites. We created a revenue share deal where we would get exposure to this traffic to help signup new members. They would get a piece of the sales generated from each of these customers. This was a win-win. They got us free marketing and they received greater monetization of their traffic.

Strong allies can save you money and make you more powerful. Maybe you could find a software development company to give you half off their standard prices because they want to establish a relationship with you when you are small. They do this in the hope of getting more of your business down the line. Think through your personal and professional connections to see if there are any that you can turn into assets for your new company.

Know your Strengths and Weaknesses

Drafting the strengths and weaknesses portion of your business plan is a good exercise in self-examination. Be as honest as possible without going overboard. This section is valuable for early partners and investors. It cuts through a lot of the fluff. They will be able to see if you have the proper outlook of your company's road map. Also, it gives vision into your shortcomings so that they can help cover your weaknesses.

What are you good at presently?

You can just look back at the other sections of the plan you have written so far. The info is there for what you must do to succeed. Which parts of it are you confident about? Highlight these traits in a list with short explanations.

What are the strengths and weaknesses of the industry you are entering? An example of industry strength is why online retail is better than brick and mortar. Company strengths would be why my online retailer is better than the other online retailer.

With your weaknesses, be realistic. If you're going into a business where you're under-capitalized or somebody has built a brand name be forthcoming. Weaknesses can also be about your idea, your industry or yourself.

Personally, I know that customer service has always been a limitation. So, I skew my businesses to require very little interaction with clients avoiding areas like mass retail. Pushing towards ones that have few customers like large consulting clients. Knowing my short comings allows me to avoid putting myself in situations where I am doomed to fail. If you understand where you're weak you will determine a way to get strong or what types of businesses to avoid from the outset.

Opportunities section is just like it sounds. What is the upside for the business? Is there new technology that will make something much easier to sell than before? For instance, advances in 3D scanning will allow selling custom clothes on the internet to become plausible for a mass market.

Threats are the counterbalance to opportunities. Something that could come along and wipe out your business or the industry. Maybe a supplier of your product is considering getting into your part of the industry and cutting you out.

Examine each of the 4 portions of SWOT. This is a self-awareness test for you and your business that will be available for your potential investors to read. It's ok to lean towards the glass half full side of analysis, but don't ignore negatives all together.

Exit Strategy: Which Way is the Exit?

The exit strategy sections I have found to be a one of the more amusing parts of business plans. In reality exit strategies are either brought to you as an opportunity or forced upon you when you have lost control. They almost always require an element that is outside of your influence.

Are you going to sell your business? Easiest and cleanest exit.

Are you going to go public? Wouldn't that be nice but going public is a pain and doesn't have the prestige it once did.

Or the worst-case scenario, you are going to out of business and liquidate. This is where you are in a business with tangible hard assets you will be able to sell and recoup some of your losses.

One thing that potential investors want to know is that you are open to exit scenarios. It is a way for them to judge your level of commitment and positivity. Also, it can help them foresee problems before they happen. For instance, if you think you have a billion-dollar company on your hands in 10 years, they would ask if you would sell in 2 years for $50 million. Sounds like a pleasant scenario, but some founders are so dedicated to their ideas that they would answer no they wouldn't sell. This could clue a potential investor in that you may not be rational down the road. On the other hand, many businesses have turned down smaller offers, to then grow mightily. (There is no one path)

Ultimately, exit strategies examine the possibilities of leaving the business. To do this you look at similar companies and industries then see what happens to startups there. I said these make me chuckle because how far they are in the future. They often show how deluded people are about their idea. I would not spend a lot of time on this because an exit strategy assumes that you understand how your business is going to unfold. Truth is you won't know till you get there.

FINANCIAL STATEMENTS

BALANCE SHEET INCOME STATEMENTS CASH FLOWS EQUITY

Financial Projections: Numbers Don't Lie?

When somebody experienced reads business plans, they likely read two things first and decide if they want to continue. The executive summary which sums up all the information inside of the plan into one page at the front. Then they skip to the end, which are the financial projections and use of proceeds.

The financial projections show the result of your plan. This is where your thoughts are reduced to cold hard numbers. How you're going to make money and spend money. Forecasts in a startup business plans typically are complete and utter bullshit. Human nature dictates that people are going to paint a rosy picture. Who would start a business and be a pessimist? Also, projections assume the world operates on a steady even keel and we know shit happens.

DBAS: Anyone can create projections that look amazing on the surface. Don't pat yourself on the back just because the documents say you are going to make money.

Even though projections are inaccurate I go to them right away. Why might you ask? This is because projections are revealing of the person who's creating the plan. If you understand your business, that will come through in the way you craft your numbers. These projections show that you understand how the business will function. We know you're not going to be able to predict the future. What you're showing is, if the future unfolds in the parameters you set, this is how the company will perform. Creating a window into your ability to correlate events as your business grows. Financial projections are giant "if then" statements. Meaning if X happens Y will also happen or need to happen. The more factors that alter your business that you can take into account, the better off you will be in the future.

The two parts of the financials to focus on are the income statement and cash flows. Yes, there is also a balance sheet but that is much simpler. The income statement is where you plot out how and when you will make or lose money. The cash flow is just as it sounds, a document that tracks how much cash you have on hand and how it will flow in and out over time. This is something too many budding entrepreneurs ignore at the outset.

Understanding that if you will be owed 1 million dollars at the end of year 2 by your customers in the income statement has ramifications. Recognizing that you wouldn't have enough money to pay your vendors if you are owed a million dollars is cash flow management. In this case, cash flow is going to become an issue in the second year and hence is something that you need to account for in the plan. For example, to solve this issue you could find someone who will buy your receivables for 97%. It may cost you 3%, but it at least shows you are aware of a potential roadblock.

Another example, your initial office has a capacity of 40 people and if sales grow as expected you are going to need a bigger office. Hence, you're going to have to expand and spend more money because a bigger office costs more money (plus moving expenses etc.).

By accounting for this type of occurrence in your financials it shows that you've thought through growth beyond a linear progression. "There's going to be an increase in sales of 10 percent every year for the next three years". Again, "if then" statements. You are creating the world as it will exist in your theoretical future in the financials. You must show that you can foresee how this growth impacts profit, spending and cash on hand. Prove that you have considered all aspects of what is necessary to make your business work.

Never go into a business where you look at the projections and say Oh God this thing will never make money. That should seem like common sense. The projections should always look reasonably good. If they don't then throw out the plan and move on to a different idea. Before you toss the baby out with the bath water, there's also the option of doing conservative or aggressive projections. Outsiders would prefer conservative but sometimes if you're going for funding, you may need to get aggressive. In my experience, most projections are done from an honorable level of trying to take the best information to create financials which are reasonably plausible Wildly exaggerated projections rarely serve any party involved. As a rule. it is always better to under promise and over deliver if possible.

Final Words:

Don't be intimidated. Put it down on paper. So when you go to talk to people you have a plan that shows this idea isn't something that you thought up this morning in the shower. Create a plan with the sections on the product, marketing, competition, exit strategy and financials. This process will help you better understand your idea and build the confidence needed as you press forward.

Chapter 10: Raising Capital

Getting the money that you need for your new business is obviously a big deal. There are lots of questions to answer. How much money do I need? From who? When should I raise it? How much equity do I give up?

From your business plan you should have a good sense of how much money you are going to need to get started. Keep in mind you should always build in room for margin of error and acts of god.

One additional question you should ask yourself is how comfortable you are with losing other people's money. It's important because some people have problems with the guilt that comes when this happens. Self-assess and determine how you'll be able to sleep at night in a negative outcome. Obviously, I'm not saying you need to be a sociopath, but you need to be somewhat detached. This answer helps dictate who you should ask for money. Clearly you are much more likely to feel bad about losing grandma's retirement account than a billionaire's angel investment. This is a little bit pessimistic but hope for the best and prepare for the worst.

Who's Got Cash?

The next question we're going to ask is, who are you going to raise the money from? Each option has its pros and cons. What are the goals of each of the groups of potential investors? What would they call success for the investment? How much involvement in operations or decisions would they have?

Venture Capital- Friend and Foe

If you need millions to get going venture capitalists are the people with deep pockets. Most are going to look to put in a minimum seven figures. Venture capitalists are looking to hit big. Their goals are going to be for you to own the market, to go public, to have a massive exit. As stated earlier, VCs are playing a numbers game. If they make (10) $1 million investments, their hope is that one of them will be worth $50 million. Their goal is not to make a reasonable profit in each investment but for most to fail while one or two to crush it. Hence, they will be pushing you to run your business in a go big or go home fashion.

It would be nice to dominate an industry and have a $100 million company or even bigger. However, this path isn't usually organic and even keeled. VCs will also look for a say in the way you run your business. Help you hirer key positions and have multiple seats on your board of directors. There are varying types of VCs with different methods of operation. Do your research on the investments they have made in the past and how they have turned out.

DBAS: These people aren't your friends, they are seasoned investors who look at you like a commodity. Don't be seduced by their sunny outlook because they will cut your heart out if it makes them a few extra shekels. If you're not going after the big money in an absolute sprint, then VCs aren't the way to get started.

Will you be my Angel?

Angel investors are wealthy individuals who are looking to invest in businesses, but don't invest for a living like VCs. This could be anyone, but high-income individuals with decent wealth usually make the best angels. Doctors and lawyers are often a big part of this segment. People who have enough money that they're willing to get risky where they invest. They probably have a significant amount of money in standard investments and are looking to be speculative. Some do it just to be a part of something. For a story to tell at cocktail parties.

Most are not likely to miss the money that they are using for the investment. Investing with you is not going to change their plans in life at all. These people are putting up to the five hundred thousand level, but that is malleable based on how much you are looking for in total.

The methods of finding angels has advanced with the growth of the Internet. There are sites like angels list where you can go see active angels. Also you can find meet-ups and groups for angel investors. Local "Shark Tanks" that get together a few times a year. Just poke around the web and you will find some.

As with any investor, be aware of the angel's goals and personality. What is their knowledge of what you're doing? What are their expectations on timetable of return on investment? Do they expect to be involved in decision making on any level? Also get to know the individual and see if they mesh with your personality. If things go well, you are going to have to deal with this person for a long time.

Crowd Funding

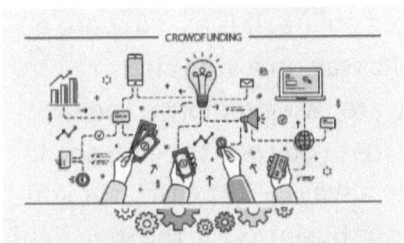 Crowdfunding sites allow you to raise capital by amassing smaller contributions from a large group of people that you don't have direct contact with. These are sites like Kickstarter and Gofundme. This option does depend on what your business is going to do.

Crowdfunding is much easier if you are producing a consumer product. If you're going to be building a product that requires a lot of capital, it's a good way of pre-selling selling items. There are many ways to get creative to offer unique tiers of investment level. One of the more interesting ones I encountered are people who were trying to fund a movie. They offered someone an Executive Producer credit if they give enough money.

This is a viable method, but people are becoming wary because crowdfunding doesn't always work out for the buyer/investor. Some companies take money and don't deliver a product in the end. There is little protection against fraud or negligence.

It's worth looking at if just to see what other companies are doing and how they are structuring their offerings. And if you don't have access to other methods of raising money.

Online equity

The loosening of securities laws has opened new ways of raising capital. A few sites have sprung up that allow you to offer equity in your business online. It is as if it were a private offering, but in a public way on a web site. Seedinvest.com and Republic are two examples. The laws are changing fast, make sure that you read the fine print. These methods may seem like a way to fast cash, but you don't want to contaminate your business for the long haul.

Friends and Family: Tried and True

Friends and family are not much different than angels. You are going to people that can afford the investment. They ALWAYS should be able to afford the investment. Too many bad TV reality shows display people who have talked their mothers, fathers, aunts, uncles, grandparents into investing in a business that goes the wrong way. It ruins their lives and their relationships.

Friends and family are going to have a soft spot for you. These are people who want to believe in you and your bright future. Do not take advantage of this. Seriously, if you learn one thing from this book don't risk your bond with the people you love over money. It's ok to get them to invest, but don't delude them or let them invest more than they can afford to lose.

In my very first company, I took an investment from both my parents. Five thousand dollars a piece and it was not going to ruin their lives if I failed. I also raised money from school friends and other people that I that I knew reasonably well. Small amounts of capital from a handful of people that knew me and believed in me. The difference between friends and family from angels is from where their belief stems. Friends and family are investing because they believe in you and want to see you do well. They won't ignore the validity of the concept, but they are less focused on the business idea than angels.

Don't let your enthusiasm get the best of you. Money complicates things. My first startup, where I did raise money from friends and family was successful. That was nice that I was able to return a profit to these people. On the flipside, it did mean that they were all up in my business. At times when we were growing fast, I got a sense that some of my friends and family were letting their expectations get out of whack. Failure brings out one type of emotion, success brings out another, which is greed. This can mess up your relationships just as fast as failure. Proceed with caution.

Bootstrap: Pull Yourself Up

The last method people use to capitalize is bootstrapping. This is simply using your own money. I know it's a very difficult thing to do. Each one of the other methods that I've named has its downsides. Losing your own money is probably the easiest way to go if you can afford it. Bootstrapping works well because it will light the fire under your ass to go out and attack the business. This is often used for the very initial stages, while you are looking for other methods of capital.

If you don't have enough money to bootstrap yourself at all you've got to ask yourself why. Why do you find yourself flat broke and totally incapable of starting a business? That might be a red flag that you shouldn't start your own business.

DBAS: Bootstrapping only lasts so long and isn't meant to be a long-term solution.

Most businesses are going to hit an inflection point where they need a capital infusion. Which will have you following the other methods I have laid out. But if you can bootstrap for a little bit, it's a good idea because you don't have to deal with investors right away. Focus entirely on your idea and gaining basic momentum. All the decisions are yours to make without having to consider any outside forces.

DBAS- This doesn't mean you should risk your entire life savings. Let's say no more than 25% of your worth should get tied up in the launch of the business. The younger you are the higher this number can be because you have more time to build your fortune back up.

What comes with the money?

If you're going to take money from investors you should ask yourself what comes along with the cash. Are there other ancillary benefits or detriments that investors bring with them. Capital can be found in a lot of different places as we have talked about here. What you want is money that comes with something extra.

- Do they have connections that will be helpful?
- Do they know influential people who will help you succeed?
- Do they have a strong personal brand that adds credibility to your venture?
- Do they have experience in the industry you are in?
- Have they successfully sold a business?

Leveraging these advantages can be along the same lines as a strategic partnership. Somebody who's already in the industry and they're looking to invest in you. By working with them you're already advancing along the path you want to see. Getting in the door, along with getting the money. Look at the challenges or weaknesses your company is facing and ask yourself if this potential investor can help solve them.

Look for investors who have experience in the area you're operating. Maybe they're not strategic partners, they don't know anybody specifically to put you in contact with but they're going to be an advisor. Somebody who has had a lot of business success. You can look to them to help mentor you at different times. There will be situations that come up that are universal to all businesses. Having access to someone with experience will only help you find your path quicker and cheaper. Don't underestimate having someone who has been through it before in your corner.

Baggage Capital

Be aware of the baggage that comes with capital as well. For example, if you take capital from a strategic partner, the downside could be locking yourself too much to one company. I have signed deals that raised cash and made an investor my exclusive supplier. This left me with fewer options down the road and less leverage in future negotiations.

A good trait that you can look for in an investor is one who will just leave you alone. This goes across all methods of raising capital. People who want to meddle in your business and want to constantly know what's going on are a pain in the ass. That will take you eye off the ball and cause unneeded anxiety. This doesn't mean that people who want to know what's going on in the business are wrong, bad or any of those things. You should have some sort of formulated reporting so that they can get answers to questions without having to ask. If you give no info to your investors, they will think positive things until they don't. Then they will panic and barrage you with requests.

Side Note: Get Out in Front of It

For many years I would send out a monthly letter to my shareholders explaining what had happened that month and what we see happening the next month. I wasn't required to do this in a private company. Doing it, kept people off my back and by volunteering information I didn't have to worry about it for the next 30 days. A simple short letter or email will suffice.

People who don't bother you are more important than you might give credence to at the outset. You will likely be so excited that someone wants to give you capital that you figure you will worry about the rest later.

DBAS: You don't want somebody showing up in your office and asking to review the checkbook.

I'm speaking of nosy people with too much time or too little trust. If there's a legitimate reason they're showing up then you might already have a problem, but we will burn that bridge when we come to it.

Money Doesn't Come Easy

Something to think about when you're raising capital is it's usually a continuing process. It's not like you go out to the money store and get all the capital you'll ever need. They're likely going to be multiple rounds and multiple valuations. Basically, rinse and repeat this process.

The best way to deal with this is keep your house in order. Don't be lazy about the investor paperwork. Create a shareholders rights agreement which lays out the corporate governance. (Get this from one of the many websites that offer it and keep it simple.) Carefully file all the investor paperwork where people signed their shareholders agreements to invest.

Make sure you build a working cap table. This is the document that shows who owns what shares in your company. Also keep your cap table as simple as possible. I like to make a spreadsheet and anytime the cap table is updated I make a copy of that sheet. Then name the newest tab with that day's date. This creates a working record of where your cap table is and how you got there.

It's also likely that you will employ multiple methods of raising capital. You could start with bootstrapping, advance to friends and family, next angels and then head for the VCs after that. This is just a part of doing business.

The Equity Dilemma:

Don't Throw Too Many Gold Bricks Off the Plane

Getting money from investors is a euphoric feeling but be careful when you're raising capital that you don't give away too much equity. If you believe in your company, you want to raise as little money as you need and retain as much of the ownership as possible.

The way that I've always visualized equity in a startup company is like you're on a plane on the runway about to take off. The entire plane is stuffed with gold bricks (Your equity being the bricks made of gold). The puzzle is to figure out how many of those gold bricks you must throw over the side in order to get the plane light enough to take off. You want to throw exactly as few gold bricks over the side as humanly possible. Yet, you'd rather end up with 10 percent of the gold than a plane that crashed.

Be mindful when you throw them overboard because you can't make more. Once they are gone, they are likely never coming back. At the outset you will be shedding gold bricks to investors, partners and employees. All of this in the hope of getting that plane flying high in the clouds. You need to get the plane off the ground. It's a delicate balance. Greed has killed far too many companies. Being able to navigate these types of high wire acts is what being an entrepreneur is all about.

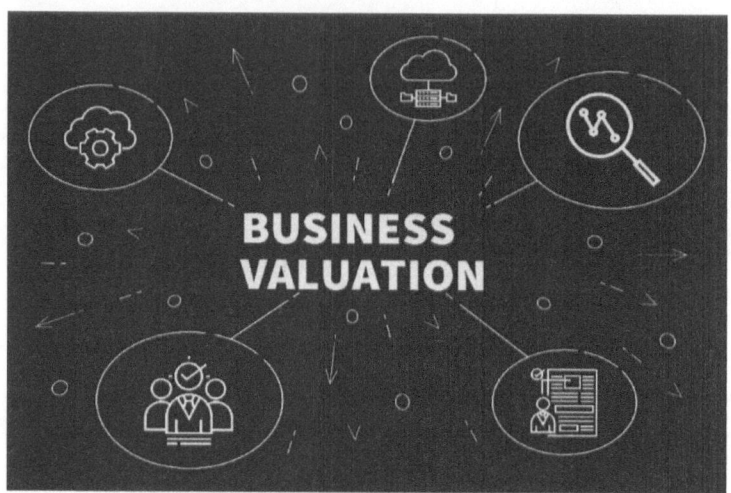

Valuing your company: What's the price of your gold bricks?

When you're looking at deal structuring your mind will almost always go directly to the valuation. That's one of the great mysteries of starting a business and raising capital. How much to value your company at when raising cash. What is the price of your gold bricks?

Sadly, there are no magical answers to valuation. Like anything else in this world your equity is worth exactly what someone is willing to pay for it. Some businesses are a little more straight forward and have existing models. If you're opening a liquor store and you have done this 3 times before. You have a pretty good idea of what the business is worth. You're going to do X business per year and you know the profit margin, you know the investment etc. There is less imagination needed to see the success or failure. The celling and the floor of the investment is narrower.

It takes more vision to see the upside of most businesses which are starting from the tiniest ACORN.. Let's says you want to build an app that sells plane tickets to people who want to fly first class. You can examine the market and your projections from your business plan to create a viable valuation. You do this by seeing how much profit you will make after a few years. You will also be able to see how much money you will need to get there. To come up with a price you must think about the risk of failure vs the return on the upside. Put yourself in the shoes of your potential investor. What return would you need to make for the risk to be worthwhile?

The earlier on you are in your startup the harder it is to create a valuation. You have very little hard data. As you move along, and things go from theoretical to empirical, it gets easier. If you've ever watched the TV show Shark Tank (which I recommend for budding entrepreneurs) it is entertaining to watch people try to create a valuation for a company which has never sold anything or done much at all. You will notice that these are the types of negotiations that have the largest swing in amount asked for vs what they end up with.

During the valuation process remind yourself of ancillary benefits that these potential investors bring. You're going to want to value your company, your old gold bricks at the highest price possible. Investors are going to want to pay less. Duh. The ultimate question is, "by taking this capital am I going to make more profit in the end?"

The very first company I started we valued at $150,000 and we almost sold that company for $50 million 5 years later. In fact, we almost sold it for $3 million, sold it for $10 and then it was sold for $15. The point being we undervalued ourselves initially and made profit for a lot of people. Yet if we had valued our company at more, we might not have gotten investors and never gotten the plane off the ground.

DBAS: Be slightly greedy when it comes to valuation. But be realistic.

Price is going up!

If you do multiple rounds of funding, you will end up with people who own stock at prices that are different. This creates investors who have varied points of view. In the example above, there were people who bought in at a valuation of five million. That is 30x the price of the original investors. The group that bought in at $5 million ended up losing money. This is because the company exited after 15 years of business didn't produce five million dollars in profit from the time that they entered. The people who got in early made over 20x their investment.

As we dealt with different options of exit strategies, it was simple to see that one group of people was very happy and the other not so much. This is bound to happen with your company if it grows over time. The goals of investors will be varied based on when they got in and at what price. It's worth noting here that trying to maintain a controlling interest in your company makes things much easier. If you have over 50% you ultimately can make the decisions.

Valuation is going to be a moving target based on where you are in the process. People talk about down rounds, a point where the value your company has decreased since the last funding. That's a bad thing on the surface, but business is a game of survival too. Don't let pride or greed cost you the chance to stay alive. You want to build a company with growth. Something on a solid footing that can produce profit.

Valuation should come from your projections combined with other examples that you may be able to find in public documents. Try and look at other companies in the industry, but they probably are further along in the business cycle than you.

Creative Capitalization: Oh You Fancy.

Given the fact that the valuation is subjective, you must be willing to be creative when it comes to making a deal. This means thinking of things beyond shares in your company that you can give as part of the deal.

The Best of Both Worlds

One of my favorite methods is a combination of equity and debt. Making the investment part loan and part stock makes it more palatable for investors. Essentially, individuals want to know if they put $100,000 in your business, how are they going to get their money back. The investor is worried that it will take too long to get paid back or the money will get diverted to other areas. If they get 10 percent equity for their $100,000 and the company's going to make $200,000 the first year. They're going to get $20,000 back that year and that's if you distribute all the profits. At that rate, it's going to take five years for them to get their money back.

Your company needs that $100,000 investment to get to the $200,000 profit. The investor could ask for more equity like 20%. But you may not want to give up that much stock. This is where a hybrid of equity debt is a solid solution. You can create a structure where the investor will get paid their money back first before profits are distributed. In the example above in the first year they would get their $100,000 back plus 10% of the remaining $100,000 profit. Or you could also spread the loan payment out over a period of time. Let's say 5 years in this case. They would get $20,000 a year for 5 years plus 10% of distributed profits.

Doing a mix of equity and debt gives people a greater feeling that they're going to get return on their money sooner. Also, in this scenario they're much more likely to get some sort of return. If they just plow the $100,000 and you don't have to service any debt you may lose all the money before they ever see a penny. But if you agree to pay them back quarterly over the course of the next 5 years, it chips away at what their investment. Paying them $5,000 every 3 months they'll feel more comfortable and you won't have to give up the equity that you cherish.

Royalties: Might Just Work

You can also consider offering a royalty as part of an investment deal. This is where the investor would get a percentage of each sale. Let's say you are selling ocean kayaks that wholesale for $500. You could make an agreement to pay an investor $50 for everyone you sell. I'm not a big fan of these unless they have a sunset clause. Where the royalty agreement ends after a set period or set amount of sales. This would be where the investor was getting part equity and part royalty. Some investors could seek a pure royalty deal. I am not in favor of those types of deals. You would then have a built-in cost forever. That could hamstring you in all sorts of ways you can't even envision yet.

Check the Junk Drawer

If you find yourself at an impasse in negotiations, review other assets you have at your disposal. One deal we did was coming down to the nitty gritty and the investor was on the fence. At the time, we had a million American Express miles from putting expenses on our cards. The person doing the deal with us was a frequent traveler. In an attempt to close the agreement , I said "How about we throw in 500,000 AmEx miles?" The miles weren't something that we put great value in and it wasn't something we could convert immediately into cash to build the company. This must have struck the right nerve because he liked the idea of those 500,000 Amex miles and did the deal.

Look around your office, not everybody's going to be sitting on 500,000 Amex miles. Who knows what asset might help you get the investment for another deal. I used a website domain in a similar fashion to the Amex miles. I own a highly sought-after travel domain and we put the rights to purchase it into the contract to get it done. The deal said, the new company can have the right to buy the domain for a hundred thousand dollars. I didn't even give up the domain, just the right to buy it at a price. I committed the domain at what was a discounted price to create value. The investors liked the implied value of the option to buy the asset if they wanted . Eventually they decided not to buy it, but it made the deal happen.

There are infinite ways to get a deal that makes all parties happy. Stock, debts, royalties, assets are some of the best pieces you have to close an investment. Find what the investors want. It's there somewhere.

Fight For Your First Right

One deal point that always sticks in my craw is right of first refusal. I hate first right of refusal. This is where you give an investor the right to buy something before anyone else, given that they will pay the same price. This provision cost me more money than I may ever see. Avoid it if possible.

A $50 million-dollar deal that I was not able to compete came down to a first right of refusal provision. This clause was a throw away in an early contract with a supplier. They gave us a large advance on earnings, but as part of it they wanted first right of refusal to buy our company. Fast forward to a few years later, we got an offer on the company and this supplier exercised their right to match the offer. Then at the last minute they backed out. This spooked the original buyer and torpedoed the deal. The supplier was too large a company to attack from a legal perspective or at least this is what the lawyers told me. In this situation I was the schmuck.

DBAS: Never give first right of refusal in a contract if you don't absolutely have to or if it's not providing a lot of value.

It's a War of Attrition. Don't Get Worn Down.

Remember when you are raising funds you're going to have to be a good negotiator. You will get to a point as you're closing the deal that you just want to throw your hands up in the air and accept whatever the terms may be. You will get exhausted in the process and want to get back to running your business. Be aware of this and avoid giving in on last minute changes to get the deal across the finish line. Seasoned negotiators will take advantage of this. Doesn't mean you have to throw a hissy fit and walk out, but just don't wave the white flag.

Raising capital is winning a battle not the war.

Raising capital is not the finish line. I see way too many companies feel it's a success when they get their cash. This is absolutely wrong. It's proof that somebody has confidence in your business, which is excellent, but it is just the beginning. Likely you have not made any money at this point. Don't look at raising capital as an endpoint. It is a milepost along the way. It's ok to celebrate getting past this obstacle, but again this just means you are in the game.

Only Take What You Need

A piece of advice a billionaire gave me about raising capital I've found to be valuable is take only the money you need. Never a penny more. Back to the old gold bricks analogy, keep as many as you can to get the plane off the ground. However, someone may offer you more money than you expected because they want to own more of your company. Some investors feel they need a certain percentage of the overall business to make it worth being involved in. This creates a conundrum.

Don't take more money than you need just because you can. What you seek should include a bit of a buffer for downturns or unforeseen events. Beyond that, don't just take money because it's been offered to you. On the surface it will feel great that you have more money than anticipated. It is not hard to find ways to spend cash trust me. Yet, you may set in motion a chain of events that you hadn't intended at all.

I've been guilty of this mistake in the past. The deal I offered was a $100,000 for 5% of the business. The investor didn't want to be in this business for only 5% and countered with 10% for $200,000. In a vacuum there are good ways to handle the extra cash, but the world doesn't operate in a vacuum. This deal caused me to alter the business plan away from the original strategy. Unfortunately, it ended up tanking the company because we got too aggressive too early.

We had too much money and didn't want it to just sit in the bank (which would have been better). So, we doubled down on our efforts. What this did was create problems that were twice as large and almost impossible to solve. Had we not taken the extra money we would have moved at a slower pace. Then we probably could have caught the flaws in our plan before they grew so large.

DBAS: If somebody wants to pay you a higher valuation great but taking more capital than you need can lead you down the wrong path. Don't look at somebody offering you more money than you need or want as a god send. Yes, it is a compliment and it is worth a wry smile but stick to your plan.

Paper Tigers: Millionaires today....

I'll finish up the capital raising section with this story. At the beginning of the dotcom craze I almost went to work for another company versus starting up one myself. The company was located in Manhattan about two hours from where I was living at the time. They had maybe a 1,000 square foot office above a gym in the West Village with a dozen or so employees. It was 1998, I remember going for an interview and finding out this company was worth $500 million dollars.

The principles of the company were probably worth on paper $40-50 million. These were high flying times and this wasn't as uncommon as you would think. Low and behold they offered me a gig there, but I turned it down. In my mind I couldn't figure out how this small company with little going for it was worth so much. Part of me felt like this was a house of cards and another part felt like if they can do it so can I.

Within two years the bubble burst and they got nothing. As far as I know they made no money at all. So, you can be rich on paper. You can get an amazing valuation. You can look great, but if you can't cash out it really doesn't mean anything. Don't get focused on the value of paper that you can't cash in. This will distort your mind and take your eye of the real prize. It gets back to the idea that raising capital or getting a high valuation is not the goal. It's just a part of the process of building a great company.

Final Words: Capital is just the fuel in the tank you need to go. Raising money is an important part to starting and growing your business. Determining the value of you company and the right deal are part art and part science. Balancing the desire to maintain equity whilst having the capital you need to grow is a constant battle.

Be aware of the options that are out there. Also be cautious about who you bring on as an investor. Some bring added benefits while others can hold you back. Get the money you need to execute your plan and get to work.

Chapter 11: People to Hire

Friends, Romans, Countrymen lend me your ear. This section is about who you choose to work with in your startup. Hiring people and how to assemble your team is key. These are the people you are going to war with. Comb every possible place to find the talent that suits you. There are tons of websites like LinkedIn or Glassdoor that help you hire people. Consider people who you already know. These first few employees will set the tone for your business forever. No pressure. LOL

Hiring A's or Potential Ones

I remember I was sitting down with Bob Deiner, he was one of the founders of Hotels.com and I had worked with him on various projects over the years. While I was developing a new venture, during one chat I asked, "Hey Bob what are the cornerstones of a good business?" I had sought his council on many things over the years but had never asked for his core tenants of running a business.

He replied," The number one thing is only hire As don't hire Bs." What he meant by this is only hire great people. That'll get you where you want to go. I know that sounds simple, but if you only hire great people then you will surround yourself with excellence. If you hire people that can do the job only better than mediocre, you're never going to achieve much beyond just being mediocre.

People rise to the level of their incompetence inside of a company. Basically, they get promoted to a point in which they are in over their heads but that's something just to keep in the back of your mind.

That's an interesting thing, hiring As. It's a solid goal, but I don't know whether it's achievable. I certainly think when you're building your core team you want to hire As, but they aren't that easy to find. And even if you find them you are going to have to figure out how to entice them to join you. I'm of the opinion that you can't always hire As, but for your most important posts you must do this.

For places where you can't find top class talent look for someone who has upside. If offered the opportunity to coach two players who run just as fast as each other. One with perfect form and one with imperfect form, I'd choose the imperfect one, because they have room to improve.

DBAS: The better the people around you, the higher the ceiling your business has.

Look Close to Home: Friends and Family

When founding a company it's easier to start with the people that you know. Schoolmates, former coworkers, family, friends. Obviously, you must be weary of working with family and friends just like taking investment capital from them. Working together can destroy relationships. Yet it has substantial benefits because there will be a closeness that creates an inherent trust. I suggest friends over family simply because in life you get to choose your friends but not your family.

The first real company I founded was with one of my best friends in high school and a fraternity brother from college. Also, the first couple of people that we added to the team were people that we knew or met while in the industry. Over time I continued to try to hire people that I had known in previous businesses, friends, or schoolmates.

Former coworkers are a good place to look because you know how they act in a professional environment. There is an easiness of hiring people that you know because of existing comfort. You have had a large sample size to judge someone's skills, character, and ambition. This far outweighs what you can learn from a resume and a brief interview.

There is a downside as I mentioned before. A few of the friends I worked with our relationship ended up worse for the wear. That's just life. Most people have fewer friends as they grow older, but don't use that as an excuse to mistreat friends in business. At some point you are going to run out of people you know to bring on and you will have to move to a more traditional process.

Don't Hire Assholes

Another credo that I subscribe to and recommend is "don't hire assholes". You will spend a lot of time with this person in a startup. Their out of work life could spill over into their work life in a way that you're not comfortable. You may have to travel with this person, eat with them, and do a lot more than just work with them. I don't find it a good strategy to hire people that rub you the wrong way. You are creating an environment that you want everyone to be able to excel. Personal conflicts are inevitable, but assholes are the people who turn molehills into mountains.

A lot of time not hiring assholes maybe in direct conflict with the hire only As philosophy. This is because a lot of A's are assholes. Sales and marketing have more assholes than in other segments of the business. These jobs require people to have an ego and a palette for drama. You may need to grade people on a bit of a curve. ☺

Also, there might be a person that is an asshole, but they are your type of asshole. You could see how others could find them to be off putting but it doesn't bother you. This could turn out to be to your benefit. Outcasts can be diamonds in the rough. Main thing is don't hire people who will make your life and those around you harder than it needs to be.

DBAS: Even if they are rock stars at their job assholes will cost you too much in quality of life.

Due Diligence on Employees: Look at their whole life.

When you're a very small startup, whether you're bringing in people to be employees, partners or whatever, you should look at their life situation and not just their business talents. Can they travel on the drop of a dime? Work late if needed? Take less money when the business needs to cut costs?

I have talked about this before, when considering co-founders or core team members, someone who has long term commitments, has kids, owns a house, has sick parents or somebody who can't just move with opportunity will inhibit your chance for success. Somebody who can't just follow the money and is going to have things pulling them away at inopportune times. This sounds cruel and unfair, but I'm just pointing out concepts you should consider before making a selection.

Know what's an optimal situation for your partners and employees. Life is life and you can't turn everybody down all the time because of a minor flaw. Don't nitpick too much, but it's worth looking at their life situation. This is more about founders and partners than employees. When it comes to hiring employees there's a lot more legality to these topics and you're not allowed to discriminate based on what fits your style.

When you're founding a business, you're allowed to pick your partners in a lot more selective way. For me the optimal person is somebody who's young, single, smart and ready to slave night and day to get this done. But that comes with a bit of a downside They don't have the experience or the connections of somebody who is older or more established. Somebody who's younger and aggressive is more likely to bounce around. Just like they can move with you as you need them to, they can easily leave your company and go work for somebody else. These are the positives and the negatives to evaluate perspective partners.

DBAS: always be playing chess and not checkers. Think multiple moves ahead.

Building Through Interns

Another place that I've found as a great source to build staff as a startup are internships. Actually, other than me and my co-founder, the first two people we brought on were interns. We were in a technological field and there was a college nearby. We thought, let's see if there's anybody who's studying there that has skills that we could use. Initially they started as unpaid interns, but both eventually went on to become paid interns. One of the two became an employee for a few years. Interns are solid way to test drive talent at a low cost or no cost.

Interns have probably become an overly fished market and you must be fair with them. The smaller the company, the more the interns are going to get to do. In bigger companies they just fetch coffee and do menial tasks. Yet in businesses that I've run we've always given interns tasks that had value and that if they fail it would hurt us. I haven't really been let down. If you're smart with what you assign to interns, you can get a lot back from it.

You may want to hire just one intern or a group of them. If you hire interns in bulk, you'll probably lose a decent percentage. They will disappear within a month, but of the ones that stay, some will end up being full-time employees. Don't discount this avenue.

Outsourcing- Friend and Foe

We live in a 1099 outsourcing world. The gig economy or whatever you want to call it. It used to be that you have to build an organization by hiring full time employees. Now there's a ton of ways that you can find somebody who does a specific task for a living. Finding on demand services will be imperative to building a solid startup. Sites like Fiverr and Upwork are helpful for filling these roles.

On the surface outsourcing sounds great, but it's not as easy as one click ordering on Amazon. Especially when you get to working with people in places outside your home country. If you're in the United States and you're outsourcing to Eastern Europe or India or Southeast Asia, the time difference causes an issue for collaboration. Also you may have issues with working with people from other countries because they leave tasks half-finished or try to renegotiate in the middle of a project. There are cultural differences in what is common business practice. Check the reviews carefully before you think about hiring someone.

If the job is a finite task, like you want to hire somebody to build your website or to do a very specific project that isn't in your daily purview I find outsourcing is a good way to go. Yet if it's core to your business, you're better off looking to keep the staff in house as soon as possible.

DBAS: Learning how to outsource properly makes you more nimble and powerful. You can dip your toe in a lot of areas before committing too many resources.

Creative Compensation

Another thing to think about when you're hiring your initial group in your start up is how you're going to compensate them. Most startups don't have the cash out of the gate to pay their people what they are worth. In truth most of those people are there because they want the upside. They want to be successful if the company is successful. Building upside creatively is key to attracting talent and plotting growth properly.

You're going to structure personalized deals using elements like equity, stock options, bonuses, sliding scales and profit sharing. The more creative you get compensating your initial people the better talent you can attract without using cash. Remember that a big part is selling them on your idea. (The narrative you created earlier). Also, the fact that not only your idea is good, but if it unfolds as you expect they are going to be rewarded.

Create compensation packages in a way that gives them upside but where you are protective of the company's equity. This is somewhat linked to the gold bar analogy from raising capital. Getting people to work for under their market value is how your employees are investing in your company. Commonly called sweat equity.

Early on you don't want to over commit to a single employee because you may have to pivot away from this person's specialty. Try letting them help tell you what they think they can do for the company. If somebody comes and says they can help double the sales of your startup in a year, you say OK if you double the sales this is what I'll give you. And if you triple the sales I'll give you this much more. It won't always be this straightforward but focus on the goals of this position. Project what their success will mean to the company and then you have a basis to work from for compensation.

Salary and straight equity are the cornerstones of a compensation package, but stock options are a valuable tool as well. They aren't the same thing as just giving away equity. Options do two additional things. They require the employee to put up some of their own money to acquire the equity. Also, they let them share in the value increase of the company from the time they enter. This way they receive just the portion of what they helped build.

In theory, if they don't help grow the company the value of their options is nothing. Example; shares are worth $5 when they come on board. You offer them the ability to buy 10,000 shares at $5 anytime in the next 5 years. So, if the share value stays at $5, the options have no value. If the share value goes up to $10 those options are worth $50,000. (They buy the shares for $50,000 and sell for $100,000 creating that $50,000 in value)

Profit sharing is one of my favorite things to do for all early employees. This gets everyone tied to the bottom line. Instead of getting into the nitty gritty of giving away the company I would create a profit-sharing fund every month. A percentage of the company's profits we distributed to the employees. This allowed even lower level employees to participate in the company's success. This requires a bit of transparency because you are telling employees how much you're making every month. This is more effective after you have hit your stride than right out of the gate. Also, this is less effective in businesses that plan on burning cash for a long period of time. So, your expected path is a factor into how you build these packages.

I remember my father telling me when he hired a salesperson who was paid on commission," I hope she makes a million dollars a year." If she made a million, he probably made two million off her sales. I liked this concept. Put your employees in a position where they are going to succeed and that you're only caring about their results.

Understanding what motivates each member of you team is important. This is not a one size fits all world. How you come up with a compensation package for them is you communicating that you understand their value and goals.

Firing People: An Unfortunate Part of Life

When discussing hiring people, it's worth thinking about the polar opposite, being prepared to fire people. Hiring is an exciting process for everybody involved. You've got eager people who are interested in telling you how they're going to do wonderful things. You are growing your company and moving forward executing your plan. But inevitably you will have to let someone go. Maybe you have somebody who is not performing the way you need them to, how will you deal with it?

There are many reasons you will have to fire someone. Not just them being a subpar employee. That situation is somewhat easier than others. Often your business is going to change, and positions may become unnecessary. Say you hire a graphic designer to do all your in-house artwork but as it turns out there's a lot less to do than there used to be. Or a new service hits the market that lets you easily get things done overseas for a fraction of the price vs in-house. Now you've got an employee who for no fault of their own has become expendable. You've got to make the decision to fire them. This is not an easy thing to do and some people are better than others at this task.

TANGENT

As part of your initial core group of employees, it's worth thinking if one of these people is going to be the hatchet man? Is one of them going to be the one who's able to fire people without too much inner turmoil? Firing people is probably the hardest thing that I've had to do as an entrepreneur. Even harder than being in over my head in debt. This is because I always felt like the debt was on me and I was going to fight out of it. Firing somebody, especially if the person was being let go because they didn't fit the business anymore and not for performance, I felt like it was my failure. My mistake was being transposed on to them and I was letting them down.

DBAS: This is just business and by keeping an employee who you know doesn't fit your plans you don't help them or you.

The very first time that I fired somebody I was working for my father in his men's clothing store. We had a tailor who would come in late all the time and wouldn't get the work done on time. We'd promise customers who needed a suit for a funeral or something important that we could get it ready in time. Then the tailor wouldn't show up and made our business look terrible. After this happened too often, I told my father this guy must go. My dad agrees "OK go ahead and fire him."

I was just a pup at the time (22) and the tailor was around 50 years old. An older Greek guy, he was super sweet, but we just couldn't count on him to get the job done. It took me a bit to work up the courage, but I told him we couldn't work like that and I fired him. This hurt me inside because I felt like there was some solution to the problem that I had missed. I was bummed out for a few days. Some people aren't affected by this type of stuff, but I empathize with people I work with. I think this helps you be a good leader that people believe in. But this is one of the downsides.

The kicker to this story is a week later my dad hired him back. Turns out it was hard to find a good tailor that was reliable. It was better to have some tailor than no tailor. We stopped promising things could be done in short periods of time. (That simple solution I somehow missed.)

I went through all this emotional torture to fire this guy just to hire him back. Maybe that's part of why I don't like to fire people. But I do think that some leaders are more empathetic than others. I prefer to be empathetic because it allows me to be in other people's shoes and anticipate their needs. To be able to stay out in front of things. Whereas people who don't have any empathy usually get blindsided. They don't let things bother them, but they don't see trouble coming either.

Final Words

Finding the right individuals that match your personality and the business won't be a perfect process. You're not scouting the NFL combine here and looking at people's 40-yard dash times. Look at what their skills are and what they're capable of. But just as much as their skills, it is how they're going to mesh with you, your team, your business and where you see things going. Building a tight knit organization is a cornerstone for a solid business. These are the people who you are counting on to execute your plans so be careful.

DBAS: Hire A's and not assholes, best as you can.

Chapter 12: Where To Work

This may sound silly but where you're going to do your work is important and requires some forethought. This is not a complicated or an extensive topic but let me hit you with my thoughts. Businesses like retail shops or restaurants are going to require a physical location. In these instances, it's more about the geographical location of your business than much else. There have been many things written on choosing the proper location for a physical store, so I won't bore you with that here.

For many other businesses the world has changed with the Internet and physical locations are being redefined. If you're starting a business that's web based or that is not going to serve clients in person, you have a lot of options. You can get your own traditional office, a home office, an executive suite or you could go with a co-working space. All are worth considering.

The key to making these decisions is not looking at what your ego says or what your imagination paints but by trying to know who you are as a person. Obviously how much money there is in the bank matters as well. Clearly you don't want to spend money on something that is unnecessary. You will be spending a significant amount of time in this space so don't underestimate making it comfortable. I have experience with each of these options, so let me give you some the pros and cons.

The Home Office

Working at home or somebody's home, it's cheap. That's the reason that you do it because you're already paying the rent there. You're already paying the Internet and other utilities. If you throw a desk in a garage or an extra bedroom, you're on your way. When it comes to being affordable, obviously working out of your home can't be beat.

The pitfall with a home office is that the line becomes blurred between work and the rest of your life. You must be capable of going into a room, closing a door and acting like you're no longer sitting in your house. In your mind you're actually in an office where you can perform work and not get pulled away easily. Don't go make a sandwich or sit down to watch TV or play video games every five minutes.

Obviously if you have small children or a young family this will impact the effectiveness of working at home. The flexibility is great, but make sure you can get your work done without the family interfering too often.

House Rules

Creating rules for how much time you spend in your office is a good start. Any ground rules at all will help keep that work life balance clearer.

The way you enforce your work/play rules are up to the individual. This does depend on how you're going to approach your work life. There have been times where I've worked from home, when I was working round the clock. So, if I wanted to take a half hour off to go play video games or three hours off to go play it didn't matter because I was going to come back to work. (This isn't sustainable).

A good tactic to maximize results is creating strict hours in the home office. For example, from 10 a.m. to 2:00 p.m. lock in. Come out for lunch and then go back in for a few hours. Some people don't work well with rigid time allotments. If so, basically try to work as much as you can, go take a break and then dig back in. Try to set a beginning and end time or create a total amount of time you want to spend in the home office.

A strong method to determine the home office rules is to look at who you are. How old you are, what your life situation is and if they're going to be multiple people working there. Are they living together? This adds an extra layer. Myself and one of my co-founders at times would work out of the same home, where we were also roommates. I don't think that in the long term this works well. But in a pinch you have to make do with what you have.

If you're going to plan on trying to have a home office for a business that is going to grow staff, you better have a back-up plan. This might work for a short period of time, but you should figure out a timeline in which you go and get an actual office space.

DBAS: Home offices always seem great in your mind. Reality is different.

Co-Working Spaces

The next logical step here would be co-working spaces. These offer a unique option because they usually do more than just get you out of the house. Co-working spaces often get you amongst other people who are of similar mindset. People trying to get a startup going or operating a small business. This industry is evolving quickly with companies like WeWork going far beyond offering just workspace. Overall, shop around and look at what amenities co-working spaces provide. Standard ones have conference rooms for meetings or presentations. Some offer high end tech hardware that the whole office can share. Others have meetups, networking events and workshops to help promote and nurture startups.

Pricing on co-working space varies greatly depending on your market, the location, the type of space they offer you. The space varies from unassigned spot on a long desk, to your own permanent desk with locked drawers, to the high end which is an enclosed office. Another reason I recommend co-working is because they usually have short term leases. You can try it for three months and see how it goes. Experiment with it when transitioning from a home office by working at a co-working space a few days a week, and at home the rest of the week. No matter the outcome you will have a better idea of exactly what you need without a lot of the aggravation or investment of getting a full-blown office.

Executive Suites

The action of getting out of your house every day is important to some. If it's the first couple of months of your startup and you just want to buckle down, dig in and work, your home is great. Co-working space might not be for you because of the distractions and informality. Yet you might not be ready for a real office. An executive suite is an option that might offer the best solution for you.

The main difference between an executive suite and a co-working space are walls and environment. This option lets you go into an office and have a place to go that's not your home quickly. These suites allow an easy entry with not much BS. They are preset and ready to go. Utilities, furniture, front desk staffing.

Executive suites are more for businesses that have been operating for a while. There are companies like Regus who have executive suites available all over the world, but they are expensive. They also require longer leases of 6 months or more which hurts your ability to be nimble. There are likely local companies that offer executive suites that may be more cost effective. This option works better if you want to have a place where you're going to have client meetings, or you need front desk help. Because usually they'll provide phone answering and reception. This helps in situations where you want to project an image for your company that make it seem more professional.

These types of offices work well for established professionals that need a workspace but are usually out meeting with clients. People who may commute to an area and want a base because their home is too far way. For startups, executive suites can work when you are in between spaces or you are just flat out tired of working at home. Yet, I have found most people get them to "play business". People who feel they need an office, a conference room and someone answering their phones to feel like they are in business.

I am not a big fan of executive suites for startups. I've had a few across the country and they aren't that much better than home offices, but they cost a lot more. If you're beyond one or two people in your company, then you're going to probably want to get a regular office. So executive suites tend to be a waste of money. Unless you're at home on the phone constantly and have kids running around or dogs barking. On the surface these sound like they make sense but to me it's just mental gymnastics. People think if they get out their house they will work harder without the distractions. This is true to some extent, but if your distractions are things like TV and video games you will find them in an executive suite too.

DBAS: Avoid executive suites unless you get a great deal.

Full Blown Traditional Office

If you decided co-working, executive suites or working at home aren't for you then you're going to rent a regular old office. Natural progression will likely require that you will need a full-blown office because it will be part of how you set your culture. Yet pick the right moment for this. Know that they're not cheap and usually have long term commitments. Where you're used to renting an apartment and signing a lease for one year, a lot of office landlords want a three year lease on an office space. That's a big factor that would push me back in the direction of the co-working space and the executive suites.

Your business is a story yet to be told and you would like to be as dexterous as possible. You would prefer to not sign those long-term arrangements. A cure to this is to try and talk to the leasing agent/landlord about putting language in the contract that allows for you to get out of a lease if your business changes dramatically. Take a gander at how much empty space there is in a building. If its 95% occupied, you are less likely to get concessions, than if its 50% occupied. Be prepared for success and for failure. If things aren't going well and you can't afford the office, you want to get back in your house. Or if business doubles or triples and you've got to expand you don't want to be saddled with an office that doesn't fit your needs.

Beyond the lease

When you're considering your own office vs the other options there is more to think about than just the cost of rent. Office furniture can be expensive for stuff that's comfortable and sturdy. Most "real" offices come baron and you must furnish everything. Desks, chairs, lamps, file cabinets, surge protectors, paper towels, conference tables etc. That's why co-working space and executive offices are uncomplicated because they provide that stuff for you. If you decide you want to move to a new location, you don't have to take everything with you. If you have your own office, you're going to have to worry about getting the Internet and router set up. Security and an alarm. Cleaning. The electric bill, the water bill, the toilet paper in the bathroom. You get the point.

There's a lot that comes with your own office that if you can avoid from day one of your startup, it's probably the best thing to do. That doesn't mean you shouldn't get an office, just be aware of the effort involved. Putting the office together, all the furniture, getting everybody set up and whatnot in comparison to the other options where you're focusing purely on growing your business.

Final Words

Where you are going to work is not the biggest decision you're going to make. Yet it can set the tone for the way you're going to operate. Try not to over burden yourself with tasks outside of your core goals if you can help it. Avoid getting an office just to feel like you are in business. Think about what you want to accomplish in your workplace, what suits you best and then you will find the answer.

DBAS: Don't let your ego get the best of you. Get what you need not what you think you deserve.

Chapter 13: Culture as a Weapon

Corporate culture is where you can define your leadership model. A leader strives to create culture with fun and passion. Both have great value that can't be seen on projections. A fun atmosphere makes long hours easier. Passion makes the alarm clock sound like a starter's pistol. Spend time to breed passion in your team as best as you can.

Dress Code

Setting a culture of success comes down to utilizing what you have to your advantage over traditional settings. Start with the dress code.

How does dress code play in the culture? You can allow employees to work in clothes that are comfortable or expressive. There are many archetypes in the startup world, let your staff become the character of their choosing, just like a video game.

When it comes to dress code, I think not only do you promote who you want to be, you promote what you want the company to be. If you're not dealing with clients in the office on a daily basis, being laid back has its benefits by having a lax dress code. An environment that is more focused on the work than fashion reinforces what is important to the company. This doesn't mean that you should be ok with your employees dressing like slobs. It allows you to craft the image you want to project to each other and the world. Having your own look/style breeds passion.

Side Note: Look The Part

Look at yourself and play the part. Dress like the person that people perceive you to be.

If that's a suit and tie, that's a suit and tie. If that's a hoodie and a t shirt, that's a hoodie and a t shirt. Never underestimate the value of playing the part. If you want to be seen as the nerdy, super smart guy who has a great idea, look like the character that would be in a movie or TV show. People subconsciously like you to fit into a mold. This is about projecting who you want people to see you as not necessarily who you are. Or fuck it, dress however you want. Just know that it colors your persona.

Work Hours

If you can create a feeling that time in the office is not a chore, you will be on the right path. I've used flexible schedules in almost every company that I've run. Unless somebody was manning a post like customer service, where there had to be somebody there, I never set hours for anybody. Instead of set hours I would have people set their own goals. It would be evident who are the good people and bad people.

In truth I didn't really care how much people were at the office because I only cared about the results. Setting a small window, a few days a week that are targets for being in the office is wise. Say from 11am-2pm Monday thru Wednesday. This is for continuity sakes. If everybody is in house for those 9 hours a week it would take care of most housekeeping that would be needed.

Don't get too myopic in checking the hourly efforts of your employees. Look at the accumulation of progress and that people are hitting their mile markers. It'll be easier for you and them. Some people will want to be there from 9 to 5 and that's fine. Most successful startups require people to work more than 40 hours a week. That doesn't mean being in the office the whole time. My best work often comes at home, late at night. You want to encourage that type of behavior in your employees or your team. Let them find their sweet spot for their most productive schedule.

DBAS: Hire people who understand productivity trumps hours logged.

Meetings: Useful but Overused

Implementing a results-oriented culture is what you're going to need in a startup. It's important to hold meetings to build comradery and chemistry amongst your team. Yet some leaders over do it and this can pull people away from their actual work. Balance is the goal. For me, I used two types of meetings. A weekly core meeting and a monthly all hands meeting.

The weekly meeting was with the executive team made up of the core 3-6 people who oversaw almost everything. These would usually last an hour or two. and were held on a Monday because it would set the tone for the week. We'd revisit a person's goals from the previous week, where they are today and what's on tap for this week. These meetings showed if you are getting things done. It's not just a one on one thing, you discuss it in front of everybody. If someone isn't hitting their goals it shows how they are letting the team down. This further encourages people to hit their marks.

An effective way to motivate people is shame/hubris. If they're not going to pull their weight, they can't hide from it in the comfort of their office. If there is going to be a problem, everybody can see it. After the core meeting you can always pull someone aside and have a one on one thing. Overt criticism is better in this type of setting vs in front of everyone. Transparency is required in a results-oriented culture. Meetings can be a waste of time, but they are necessary for accountability.

Also, I find a monthly all hands meeting to be valuable. This depends on the size of your company because if you get big it's hard to find space or time to do this. The format of the meeting is basically a State of the Union. What happened over the last month and where are we going in months to come. Aiming to keep your team informed and engaged. Again, transparency is key to gaining trust with employees. And if employees trust you, they will run through walls for you and the company.

During the second part of these meetings I required every single employee to ask a question out loud. The size of your team again comes into play because this method could run a long time. Adjust it to fit your size and style. Do your best to keep it fun and moving along. By forcing people to ask questions, they become engaged. This makes them listen to everyone and not zone out. They don't want to ask questions that have already been posed. Most people don't want to sound like a moron. The better question they ask, the better they look in front of all their peers.

Transparency is on full display here because people see that if you get asked a direct question, you give a direct answer. Often you have teams who are in their own world and aren't aware of everything going on elsewhere. People are curious by nature and want to know what is going on at their company Often the questions would be very narrow in scope and had nothing to do with the department in which the employee worked. This is a great exercise as a leader because you are required to not only answer these questions but be able to explain it in a way that a layperson could comprehend. Results come in a culture of transparency and trust. Meetings are a great spot for these two things to be reinforced.

Vacations/Off Time

Setting your culture through vacations and off days is another way to distinguish yourself from other companies or traditional work environments. I didn't track vacation days for the core team. It wasn't important to me. Unlimited vacation days has become vogue over the past few years. I have been doing it for 20 plus years. This has been a valuable tool for a driven, results-oriented person. Vacation days don't matter because they're going to let their results speak for themselves. And that's what you want out of an employee.

If people want to take a vacation who are getting their stuff done why would that be an issue? People who are behind, it's going to be evident that they shouldn't be taking a vacation. Good employees can self-govern. The same is true of personal and sick days. If you are running a results-oriented model, the team must hit their goals. This way you are keeping your eye on the prize instead of trying to enforce antiquated rules. You may be surprised that if there is no system for them to try and game, they will be happier and more focused.

If you learn that your business has any demand spikes or seasonality you can use this knowledge to your advantage. I found that the winter holiday time in the U.S. is incredibly low for productivity from Thanksgiving to New Year's. Throughput dropped for our core business, this was the slowest sales time of the year. Based on this knowledge, we closed the office every year between Christmas and New Year's. At least seven full days and often up 10 total days with weekends.

This seems expensive, that's 2% of the work year. This was just simple logic. I wasn't getting much performance so instead of it being a negative for the company, I used it to create a positive culture piece. Every business is not going to be able to do that, but because you have your own rules, you can leverage the system to fit your peaks and valleys.

Building Bonds Amongst Your Team

In creating a results-oriented culture, team member bonding increases chances of success. If people can have a relationship that transcends the piece of work in front of them, you will achieve more. You can't just interact in the office to develop comradery. In my experience, creating formal and informal company outings help facilitate this growth.

For example, informal outings would be something like poker night, happy hour, hiking, yoga class, or nightclubs. Whatever people are into in your company. The age of your team matters and their responsibilities outside of work. Try to balance these outings to make it fit a variety of schedules.

Another way I tried to bring people together was to take the whole team out to lunch. I'd walk through the office around 12:30 or 1:00 and ask if anybody wants to go to grab a bite. The team got to talk, eat, have a good time and get to know each other. With no hours set and no limits on vacations people didn't stare at the clock. They knew how to self-govern. If they were behind on their tasks they didn't come to lunch. Or they came out to eat if they were willing to finish their work by staying a little bit later that night.

How about this? Thursday four o'clock on a summer day I'd ask who wants play golf. This sounds like I'm a cruise director here. Well, a little bit of your job as the company grows can be the ambassador of fun. That is to keep your people motivated, happy, and excited. You're building trust in a results-oriented culture. Take over a golf course for a few hours and don't break the bank. Doesn't have to be fancy to build the camaraderie. This is just an example that fit the company I was running. Read the room, know your people and what would help them blow off some steam.

DBAS: Happy employees perform better. They care more. Invest in their enjoyment of life.

For formal company sponsored outings we would hold corporate poker tournaments. These have come in and out of vogue, but they are a great way for people to interact.

We would do it during the day, so it was easier for everyone to enjoy carefree. We would go out and get tons of food and drink. We'd buy prizes like I-pads, flat screen TVs, or whatever it may be. All different types of people who come from various parts of the company who didn't interact often could have fun with each other.

You don't want to make it too stuffy or corporate. And I did find that the bigger we got the harder it was to do these types of events. So, as you grow you may want to make these outings subsets of your company.

Corporate Retreats

In a few of my businesses I utilized corporate retreats to help foster team building and carve a positive culture. One company on our fifth anniversary, we took anybody who wanted to go to Montreal. Our HQ was in the northeast part of the United States, so it was a short flight. We put everyone up in a nice hotel. (We were in the travel business, so we were able to control costs well.)

The company was performing strongly and growing fast. We wanted to show our employees that we cared and that the future was bright. For sure there are people who would rather just have those dollars in a paycheck every week. Yet, it's just not the same. We want to keep this feeling of an adventure going. This wasn't a structured retreat with talks and seminars. This was more of like a group vacation. People would explore the city during the day and we would meet up for dinner and nightlife later on.

The first retreat worked so well we decide to do it again the next year. This time we chose Miami as the destination. Guess what? It wasn't as fun or valuable. Taking your whole team on a retreat can be a giant nightmare. Trying to figure out who can go when, who wants to go where, who wants to do what is juggling a lot of balls. This was not nearly as simple as taking everybody golfing, putting on a poker tournament, or hiring a yoga instructor. This became so overwhelming that I got physically ill after the first night and hopped on the next plane home. Thankfully the C.O.O. was able to salvage the trip and get value out of it for the company.

The lesson I got was that just because an event worked one year doesn't mean you should do it every year. We should have waited another 5 years to do this again.

DBAS: If you decide to do a retreat, make one person responsible for all decision making and present it as a take it or leave it. You can't please everyone and no matter what lengths you go to, some people will not be grateful.

The bigger that you get, the harder it will be for you as an individual to influence culture. That's why as you build an organization the culture must be present in your team. So, they can try pass these values along to all the new people that you'll be bringing on.

Final Words:

Culture defines your journey and the people who come along. You should look at all the elements that you can leverage to make working at your company better than working somewhere else. The culture should match your mission. Some of these methods have become more normalized, with less strict hours, more telecommuting, open vacation time, and relaxed dress codes. These are all things that people have begun to expect. So, what are the new things that you can leverage? That is up to you. Create trust through transparency with a real human bond and the rest will take care of itself.

Chapter 14: Cart Before The Horse

Many people start a business with the goal of getting someone to buy it to make them rich beyond their wildest imagination. DBAS: Don't build to sell. It's very tempting to think about the exit strategy before doing anything. It's a mistake. You are putting the cart way before the horse. Execute your plan first, and good things will happen.

You're better off doing something very well before trying to scale with little efficiency or defensible positions. This sounds like simple behavior, but people can get ahead of themselves. You can have the idea to go worldwide but get it right somewhere first.

DBAS: Don't let your vision get in the way of the execution.

Get it Right Somewhere

An example of this concept is my company created travel guides for major tourist destinations. We were going to expand to 600 cities, but the key was to build a replicable template. Knowing what travelers wanted to learn and how to make money from it. We started with five cities to try and find that model. We picked locations that had different characteristics such as layout, size, type of tourist attractions and levels of competition. Through this we were able to understand which types of content would give us the highest return. This allowed us to pick the future destinations in order of the most profitable.

Learn your model before you scale and then grow before thinking of selling. Figure out how to learn and perfect your model as you expand. Do this by having measurable goals and data that you can review as the plan plays out. It's OK to want to sell your business as an exit, but that should come from building a good business with strong revenue or valuable assets.

Being Prepared for An Exit is Good Business

Preparing your business to be sold is different than wanting it to be sold. Your business can be exit ready by running things the way you should. Don't be sloppy. Keep good records and have accounting in order. All your checks, tax returns, expense reports, etc., are kept in a standardized way. If it came time for a sale then it would be easy for somebody to come in from the outside to understand. That is the added benefit. The true value is making it easy for you to know where your money is going. If you have a question about any of it, finding the backup information should be simple given you have a system in place.

Be diligent in protecting your intellectual property. Patents, copyrights and trademarks should be filed appropriately. If you're in a web-based business and you have domain names, be able to show the path of registration and ownership for those. So, you can prove that they could be transferred. Keeping good clean records is smart business and it will be an enormous help if you ever get to the point of a sale.

DBAS: Keep your books in order. This helps you day to day and will keep you ready if a sale comes along.

Focus on your path to profitability.

There are instances in which you can sell a business where you're not making a profit, but usually that has to do with spending more money on user acquisition. This would be because you want to gobble up as much market share of an industry as you can. Most businesses simply want to make a profit and do so as soon as possible. You want to put a dollar in the change machine get more than a dollar back. Then repeat, repeat, repeat, repeat.

Find the profit centers of the business and break them down into smaller pieces. Find ways to refine and reinvent these items. Profitability may come in a giant swing like hitting an oil well, but the effort to get there is incremental. They say the harder you work the luckier you get. Maybe, but the better you are at finding profit where others don't, the more likely you are to be successful. These edges are what will help you build a business that someone wants to buy.

Scalability Building Blocks

If you have figured out how to make a profit, the next step is to build a structure that can handle expansion. Potential buyers will come to look at the people that build up your organization. By hiring the right team of people who can handle growth, you will create a business that can be scaled. If you do strike oil, you can take advantage of it by growing it fast because the right process was in place.

Organizational structure and standardized processes are two tools to use here. People should easily know who is responsible for what and how the chain of command functions. An open-door policy of letting an employee talk to you or other core members about an issue is wise, but that's for something outside of the norm. There should be a clear flow of information. This creates an efficient work environment which in turns allow you to grow properly.

These concepts might seem unnecessary on day one of your business and they likely are, but if you wait too long to put them in place you will spend more time chasing what is happening than making things happen.

The Unknown: Outside Forces May Offer Opportunity for an Exit

A sale should be a byproduct of a good business, but you could get lucky where you build something someone else needs. Somebody out there decides they should buy a company to enter a market instead of building their own. They want to buy what you have so they can be in a market faster.

An issue can occur if you're not building something that can make a profit or is not making a profit. The leverage will be in the hands of the person who wants to acquire you. (If you don't have plenty of cash to make it to profitability.) Building assets has value and can lead to a sale, but if you have a good core business which is not in need of a cash infusion you are in a stronger negotiating position.

Selling a Business is a Pain in The Ass

People only think of the Scrooge McDuck piles of gold when considering selling a business. Let's say by the grace of all that is good and holy somebody comes to buy your company. It's an arduous process, it is not like going on Amazon and with one click a few days later a check shows up.

The more someone needs or wants you, the easier the process will be. If you invented something that the whole world needs, you will probably close the deal fast. Don't count on this.

In a standard business, the deal will start with an offer sheet or a letter of intent. Basically, an outline of a deal "we're going to pay 10 million dollars blah blah blah" and then you're going to go into due diligence. I've been through five due diligence processes and they are never fun. The buyer will hire an accounting and/or a law firm to handle this. They come in and go through all those records that we just talked about you keeping in order. They'll interview you and your staff to understand the business and the people. This is just the fact-finding portion.

The process has been likened to a corporate colonoscopy and no one enjoys it. You feel like you're on the hot seat, that the goal of the due diligence firm is to find whatever's wrong. They want to make sure that they looked at everything. If somebody buys your company that they're not making a mistake. And at the very least are operating with all the pertinent accurate data to make a decision.

If you have any skeletons in your closet they will come out during this stage. Some people try to hide issues. Others offer them up to save time figuring they will be found. Dealer's choice on this one. If it's so bad that it might kill the deal think how likely it is to be found out. If it is not a deal killer then don't worry about it. Just be honest when asked questions and you will be fine.

This process is zero fun and will suck time away from your core business. Which is another reason to not build to sell. Because if that is your ultimate goal you will be welcoming pain.

Side Note: Don't Get Brain Raped

During due diligence you give the acquiring company full access to all of your info. Some companies will enter acquisition talks just to get a look under your hood. This makes it hard to protect intellectual property. They want to know the secret sauce of how you got to be successful to a point where somebody wants to buy you. Give them enough to want you, but not enough to hurt you. That's a hard thing to balance especially if you're in an intellectual property heavy business. You don't want to reveal the magician's secrets.

There's a great scene relating to this in the HBO Show Silicon Valley, where a company pretends to be interested in acquiring another company. They used the term "Brain Rape" where the fake aquistioners put their engineers into the room for the takeover talks. They bombard the startup with questions to learn about the secret sauce. Before they realized what was going on they had given up way too much info. Don't let this happen to you.

If somebody is going to pay a lot of money, you're going to have to show them your worth somehow. Keeping your ego in check can be difficult during these processes. You're likely proud of what you've built. You could thump your chest and show people how smart you are, but don't.

Revealing your intellectual property diminishes the value of your company and decreases the likelihood of this or any other deal from happening.

During my first due diligence, I was being interviewed and I'm going on and on answering a lot of questions. Telling them everything I could think about on the topics posed.

My C.O.O. Richard, who I've stolen so many lessons from in this book, was sitting with me. (Thanks Rich). During a break he turned to me and asked, "Do you know what time it is?" And I replied "yeah it's 12:45". He answered "No, I asked you do you know what time it was?"

The answer to that question is yes or no. The point being is that people were asking me questions and I was giving them more than what they asked. When it comes to due diligence answer the question that has been asked. Don't provide anything beyond that because it will just lead to more questions.

Earn Out Burn Out

A sale isn't just a sale of your company, it is a sale of you and your future. During the end stage of the process you will get questioned by the acquiring company "How do they know that you're not going to take the money and go to the beach?" (Going to the beach is the simple euphemism for leaving the company and not looking back.

Any scenario where you are not working as hard as you are today.)

Entrepreneurs are mavericks. They're heretics. So, they don't necessarily make the best employees. The acquiring company wants to know that the business they are buying is going to continue to grow. So, they will structure the deal to keep you motivated after the sale. To this end often there is going to be an earn out clause, where they only pay a portion of the sale price at closing and the rest is paid out over the next few years.

For example, if deal calls for a $10 million price for the business and you personally are getting $5 million. What they'll do is give you half of the money upfront and then give you a third of the balance each year for three years. They also pay you a salary and possibly other forms of compensation for your work too. The earn out is not a substitute for a paycheck, but they want insurance that you are motivated to stay.

Nobody wants an earn out, only a fool wouldn't want all the money right away. Some of this is in the negotiation progress and the way you present yourself to the acquiring company. Do they feel you're just going to go to the beach or are you in it for the long haul? The weird part is these are at odds in negotiation. If you are in it for the long term, then you'd have no problem with an earn out. The key is to come up with reasons you want as little earn out as possible while coming across as you are here to stay. Bring up the fact that there may be changes in their organization and although you like them personally, you don't know if you'd like the next person that has their job.

It's a bit of bullshit coming from both sides, but you have to play the game.

These are reasons why you don't build the business to sell, if you end up exiting it's because it's the right move. Getting bosses and earn outs can be a bummer. This situation could go against why you got into this business in the first place. We started off talking about why you want to be an entrepreneur, what your end goal is or what you're trying to achieve. If it's the money, this is a way that happens. But then you could be giving back some of those other benefits of having your own company.

DBAS: If it's enough money that you never have to work again, you can always start another business. If it's not that type of money, I would think way more about the holistic idea of running your own company.

Getting Deals Over the Goal Line

Once you get through the due diligence, which is like giving birth, then the deal's got to close. Horror stories at this stage of the process are abundant. I've been to the goal line with deals a handful of times just to have them yanked. A myriad of reasons for this, but the one that sticks out was being purchased by a publicly traded company that got hit by a class action lawsuit. They didn't reveal something properly in a quarterly report and their shareholders sued. The lawsuit turned out to be nothing, but the timing caused a stop of all acquisitions. Fortunately for us as that deal was smaller than another deal that we looked at a year later.

Things can happen that have nothing to do with your deal and cause it to fall apart at the very last minute. There is a standard negotiation tactic where companies will get you to the goal line and then alter the terms at the last second. They will claim that some piece of data doesn't match up with their expectations. The strategy is that you are so pregnant with the deal that you wouldn't walk away if they dropped the price by 10% or shift the payouts a year or two longer. This is a highly effective technique and is hard to counter unless you have balls of steel. There is no way to avoid being emotionally involved once you have come this far. Try to be aware that you are likely not operating on all cylinders. You can only do your best. A bird in the hand is surely worth two in the bush.

Final Words:

You can see that you shouldn't build to sell. Build a solid, scalable, profitable business. If you build a strong company in a growth industry, I guarantee you people will come and try to buy you. Acquisitions can easily take your eye off the goal of continuing to grow. It's a lot of effort to sell your business and there are no guarantees. Just because you agree on a deal that doesn't mean it will close. Do your best to not get completely pulled away from running your venture during the process. Selling is a pain in the ass and can go wrong a hundred different ways, but hey if it's a shit ton of money

DBAS: Absent extending circumstances, take the money and run.

Chapter 15: Immature Markets Can Yield Great Upside

When starting a business and assessing your strategy I have a trick that I've learned. This is targeting immature markets. What is an immature market? It's something relatively new in the world and isn't fully formed. When an industry is in its infancy by nature it will be inefficient, and you can leverage this to make money. Additionally, large corporations are slow moving and at the outset of a market they are unlikely to be involved. This creates fertile ground for small business and entrepreneurs.

Over the years I've seen progressions in businesses, for example when Digital Marketing began it was a vast opportunity. The concept of search engine optimization (SEO) emerged. Everybody wanted to get the top of Google rankings. Then Google came out with paid advertising in search. Instead of manipulating the algorithm you could just buy your way top. Then people were doing search engine marketing (SEM) and manipulating their ads and copy to work the system. Next Facebook comes along and social media comes to the forefront with a new set of tools for market manipulation and so on.

At the beginning of each of these stages you would see an immature market. A market that doesn't understand its power, doesn't understand how to be efficient. What will become standard methodology for operating in these spaces has yet to be created. Smart and nimble companies can move fast to seize opportunity. That's something that entrepreneurs have forever been taking advantage of and it's something that you should look into. When markets are immature the profit margins are usually at their highest. As the proper techniques become understood by the masses the opportunity of exploiting these markets disappear.

Another example were web affiliate businesses. At the outset of the Internet, affiliate businesses were omnipresent and quite lucrative. You started with basics, links to web sites that would get you a piece of each sale. Next you built widgets on your site to promote the affiliate products. Then there were programs that could automatically build entire stores. Major companies building their own affiliate type sites. Affiliates became so pervasive that it led to Google banning them.

Even if you're in a market where it may seem mature there may be an immature submarket or niche. An innovation that is coming out that you can explore. This market inside of a market will be easier to exploit and that leads to higher margins.

You must identify the immature markets inside of your industry. These are the ones where entrepreneurs flourish. They are the places that have the most upside for growth. To find immature markets do research. There likely won't be many books on the topic at the inception . There may be news articles as the market grows. The best places are often website forums or sites like Reddit to find info. Hard core explorers of these new concepts usually like to find a place to talk to each other. They are also likely to share valuable intelligence.

DBAS: Making a better mousetrap is nice, but the undiscovered country is the place to be.

Trendy Markets lead to Opportunity

The optimal practices in immature markets hasn't been written yet and as the greater public becomes aware they become trendy. FOMO kicks in. People will throw money at it trying to make it work. Facebook and social media were a good example of this. Companies felt like they missed the boat and rushed to find a way to be a part of the social media scene. So, they spend a lot of capital and that doesn't necessarily work.

When the big boys start throwing big dollars at a market it can hinder the existing ways you make money, but it should open new avenues. You could literally switch sides from being an advertiser to a content provider. Instead of buying ads on Facebook or Youtube you could start to create content on these platforms because people are overpaying. Create simple experiments to find the order in the chaos. Don't prejudge or get stuck in what you think will be most exploitable. It's OK to have theories but ultimately let the data speak for itself.

When it comes to an immature market the best practices are unknown. They haven't been over fished so much that they're dead. You're want to have the ability to make mistakes. A scatter gun method is best, as they say throw a bunch of shit against the wall and see what sticks. Don't put all your eggs in one basket. You don't want to find yourself in a situation where you don't have enough crap to throw against the wall.

An example would be when people saw China as an emerging market. "We have to be in China." They go to China and try to sell their product. But what the Chinese may want to buy isn't the same as other customers around the world. If they spent all their expansion money on that first wave they'd be out of luck. Yet by dipping your toe into it and testing different ways you see how the market reacts. Then follow the data you get to explore and find the sweet spots.

Immature Inside the Mature

Just because a market is mature doesn't mean it's not exploitable. Efforts here should have a low barrier to entry because of the likelihood of failure and the need for experimentation.

Mature markets will have the most data hence they will have the most predictable path on paper. Easier for you to see your route to getting where you want to go, but the upside will likely be smaller than an immature market.

Consider that markets can grow so mature that they die, then are reborn and become immature again. The circle of life. Markets aren't just products they can be methods as well. An example I've encountered is sales by phone. At one point this was the pinnacle of sales. Yet efficiency got tighter and tighter. When the Internet came to center stage people thought that phone sales were doomed. Everyone focused on selling on the web because the cost was lower, and scalability was easier.

Companies actively sought to stop selling over the phone. What they didn't realize is that the web brought on an entirely new type of buyer . Customers who knew what they wanted to buy but weren't comfortable giving their credit card online or just wanted to hear a human voice. Especially with high dollar purchases.

Smart companies turned calls into valuable assets. Those that excelled at running call centers became extremely profitable. The whole world thought call centers and phone sales were going to die, but they became essential pieces of many highly profitable companies.

Final Words:

Immature markets create opportunities with high margins, but they don't last forever. This could be in a new technology or trend. They also can develop inside an industry that that has been around forever. Methods or sources change allowing for innovation inside of existing models. Look around to locate as many immature markets and methods that relate to your business. Set up experiments to find ways to exploit them.

DBAS: Follow the money. Be brave and might forces will come to your aid.

Chapter 16: Goals are Everything

Goals are at the core of any business or venture. Let's go a step further, goals are imperative to accomplishing anything in life. It may sound simple to say you need goals, but you need take time to make good ones. Then assess how you deal with them daily. The better you are at creating clearly defined goals, the more successful you will be in business and life.

People confuse missions and goals. Missions are more nebulous and subjective. Goals are finite and can be broken down into action steps.

Let's start with resisting the urge to create subjective goals. What success and failure are must be easily determined. Human nature pushes people toward creating goals that don't have clear results. This is because we don't like to fail, so we create a goal that is up for interpretation. Avoid this.

For example, setting a goal of "building the best product" is shitty. This is completely subjective and people may have different opinions on if you have achieved this. Like the difference between track and field and figure skating at the Olympics. One is by time, the other is by what people think. What people think is too subjective and not a powerful goal. Building the best product is more of a mission, not a goal. Missions are nice to have, but don't confuse them with goals or you are screwed.

> *"If you don't know where you're going, any road will get you there."*
> **Lewis Carroll**

How you determine your goals will likely dictate your fate. Goals should be mile markers to plot the course along your journey. This doesn't mean you shouldn't have big hairy audacious goals, just be careful that those aren't the only types you set. Goals should vary in size and time needed to complete.

Missing some of your goals is not the end of the world. It will happen. The truth is that you don't know what the future is going to bring. When you don't hit goals, having clearly defined success will help you know how far off you are. There are two sides to this. One is to know how badly we missed and secondly why did we miss. Was our effort the problem or was the goal the problem? If you set the goal improperly you may never be able to achieve it in the first place. The blame falls on the people who created the goal and not those doing the work.

DBAS: Create solid goals and you will get where you want faster and cheaper.

Goals are about accountability to yourself, the company and each other.

As I said before don't make all your goals too big. Any goal should be able to be broken down into smaller goals to find a way to accomplish it. People get overwhelmed if the goal is too broad or too big. They don't know where to start.

If you are struggling on how to do this make an outline of the process. Building a new web site that's going to be focused on e-sports? Jot down each of the broad goals. Creating a social media presence or developing brand partnerships. Then underneath each of those, list the action steps inside of it. People have the habit of feeling like if they are working hard that they are getting somewhere. Don't be fooled by this. Work smart first and hard second. This difference is in knowing your goals and action steps.

Building a new brand in e-sports as a goal is daunting until you break it into smaller palatable pieces. Stop yourself from spinning your wheels and create your outline. I need a website…. I need a logo…. I need a slogan….etc. Keep drilling these goals down till you can set up a calendar that gives you a timeline to complete the tasks that add up to your goals.

Goals Can and Should Change

Create documents or use tools that allow you to measure progress on a daily, weekly or monthly basis. Goals can and will change. That's just the way it is. There is helpful software out there like basecamp, trello, todoist and others which will memorialize your goals. This allows you to look backwards at how your goals have changed over time and why they changed. Goals can change because you missed your previous ones or maybe you have changed them because of an opportunity you recognize.

If you enter a business and say you're going to sell leather jackets, but you find out that everybody wants to buy leather wallets. You're going to change your goals because you found a new market. That's not failure, it's actually what you should do. Don't just let it happen. Be declarative when it comes to your goals. We are now a leather wallet company not a leather jacket company. Make sure you update your outline. This will help you set your future goals and allow you to create the action steps to move along this new path.

DBAS: Being stubborn is ok. Being stupid is not. Know when it's time to change your goals.

Other People's Goals

When it comes to the goals of other team members, letting people set their own goals and deadlines can be a winning strategy. If you're working with somebody who's developing the technology for your new website and they say it's going to take a month to get you all the features that's fine. Let them set that deadline because you're not an expert in that area and you need to let your people tell you what makes sense. You probably know enough to be comprehend their execution plan, but you must trust your team.

Some people be will be better at setting their own goals than others. Over time you will be able to figure out how you should adjust your expectations. That person is usually getting to stuff early or this person usually needs an extension. Some employees get too aggressive and others build in a buffer. This is human nature and you will get a feeling of why they are under or over setting their goals.

Being able to manage the goal setting of your team is part of what will make you a long-term success that can scale. Remember you can't be everywhere all the time, so you are going to have to have faith in others to grow.

R.O.B.
RESULTS OR BULLSHIT

Get it Done

A motto that I live by relative to goals is simply: **results or bullshit.** You need people who are thinking in terms of results. We're all ultimately judged on results. Excuses are like assholes everybody has one and they all stink. This is the rare time where I take a hard line. The reason is to create balance between all the freedom that my team enjoys and where we need to go. Unfortunately, in business you must be results oriented because there aren't do overs or participation trophies.

That doesn't mean you dismiss the thought process or why something went wrong. We live in a world where people say to trust the process. Even in a results oriented environment the process and results can't be fully divorced. If you go through the process the right way and come out with a different outcome than you hoped that it is ok. This is because if you repeat the proper process over long periods of time you will end up with positive results. Example: If you look both ways before you cross the street, but a car comes out of nowhere and hits you doesn't mean you shouldn't look both ways in the future.

It's OK to be empathetic and understanding of employees who miss goals. Yet you want people on your team who find a way to adapt, overcome and get what you need accomplished. If you drive home to your team that it's results or bullshit with some compassion, they will respect it.

"If you need a friend, get a dog."
Gordon Gekko

Final Words:

Setting the right goals and understanding the reasons why you made them or missed them is a road map to success. Hitting goals is how you're going to grow your business little by little, step by step.

Create documents and use tools that track your goals. Create outlines and lists that make big goals into smaller more palatable action steps. Keep focus on your objectives and adjust them as you get more info. Don't go crazy if you miss one or two but ultimately you must produce results. If you constantly miss your goals, you're not going to get anywhere.

Chapter 17: Follow the Data. Analytics Drive Your Business

Data tells you a story of what is going on in your company. Ignore it at your peril. Past generations of entrepreneurs didn't have access to as much data as we do now. This change in the overall business industry has forced entrepreneurs to become data scientists. Track everything that is reasonable as this will allow you to find honeypots. The more pertinent data that you look at the more that you'll be able to see inside of your business. Find the items that are creating the most profit and that are most exploitable. Obviously the other side where things are losing you money can be fixed or cut off.

Data lets you take your business instincts and turn them into actionable form. Seeing things that don't jump off the paper using base level stats. Like finding the true reasoning why Sundays are the highest sales day for your business. You have some theories, but you need hard proof to take advantage of this.

Back in the Day

As a younger man I worked in my father's men's clothing store. When I think back to that business if I could have done one thing differently, I would have tracked how many people walked in the door every day. That business generated customers using radio advertising, print media, word of mouth and good old foot traffic. No one was thinking about how many people walked in each day and how that corresponded to the amount of sales.

If I knew this number, then I would have been able to chart the day of the month or the weather. From this I could have determined which advertising was working best or if sales were driven by when people got paid on the first and the 15th. If this data showed the average spend of a customer on the 1st and the 15th is higher than say the 7th or the 25th I would target those days. I could alter my radio ads to be played twice as much around these dates. Also double the size of my ads in print during those two weeks and make the off weeks smaller. Effectively spending the same money but in a more efficient way. All because I had tracked how many people walked in the store each day.

Beyond Counting Customers

Back then you ran promotions by feelings and just saw how things went. There was some analysis of year over year sales data, but that was only one data point. When we ran "sales", I could have looked at what the average spend was vs. days with regular prices. Or the average profit during a sale versus a normal time. Reviewed the value of a customer during Christmas versus the value of a customer for Easter. Allowing me to alter my ad spend, inventory and staffing accordingly.

We used to just look at a customer as they walked in and tried to get as much money out of them as we could. We didn't give much thought into how they got to us or what our customers had in common. There wasn't a lot of science to it. It was all seat of your pants, but that doesn't work in the current world. There's so much data at your fingertips you must take advantage of it, or your competitors will.

DBAS: Be open to using data to make decisions. Even if numbers aren't your thing.

Data isn't always ready to eat.

One of my businesses we were selling a lot of hotel rooms online. This was early on in the evolution of the web, we did a lot of analytics before they were common place. At this time, people were tracking "hits" and other kinds of nonsensical data for a web site. You had almost no way of knowing how many unique visitors you had. The tech didn't exist to exclude bots and spiders.

There were so many search engines crawling the sites. On the day Google or Hotbot would come through to spider your website, the traffic would spike. We had to find the signal inside of the noise.

This is going to happen where you have noisy data which you will have to manipulate, or you will use it incorrectly. You can throw your hands up and say forget it, this data is crap. But you should find a solution to cull the good info from the bad .

We began to interpret and interpolate the numbers. Scrubbing it for extraneous factors to make the data more useful. Bad data can be worse than no data at all. This takes a little bit of smarts and good business instincts. Reminds me of trying to beat a video game. You learn a little each time you attempt to beat a level and eventually you gain enough experience to defeat the end boss. Fight the good fight to find the worthwhile data.

KPIs your window into performance.

All this work with the data is done with the goal of coming up with KPIs, **key performance indicators.** These are a handful of stats which are most important to your business, the drivers of your success or failure. The first numbers that you're going to have to look at each day to see if you're making progress or if there's a problem.

Big deviation in your KPIs means things are getting out of whack. Think of them like the smoke detector for your business. When they hit certain levels, alarms should go off. KPIs that I have found useful in web based businesses are cost per visitor, spend per visitor, close percentage, abandon rate, revenue per call. I could go on and on, but you need to identify the stats that provide the most direct window into your operations.

People use gross numbers too often like total sales or total visitors. These numbers are important to your cash flow and P&Ls. They don't explain trends though. KPIs allow you to home in on a problem quicker. Same goes if there's an opportunity to take advantage of, you can uncover it faster with the right data.

Create KPIs for each level of your sales funnel. A sales funnel is the process that a customer goes through to buy your product. Take a look at the sample funnel below. You would want a KPI for each level of the funnel.

Looking just at sales figures, you might accept a problem as just variance and not be alerted to a specific issue. If you are also looking at KPIs like average spend per customer, this might show that people are spending much less money per visit. Then you can look at the average time someone is spending on the site and see if the spend drops corresponds to the time spent. If they correlate you know you need to focus on keeping people on the page more. If they don't correlate you can look at the conversion process and see if anything has changed. Maybe someone in your company changed the checkout form or moved the add to cart button. KPIs are the clues that allow you to solve the case.

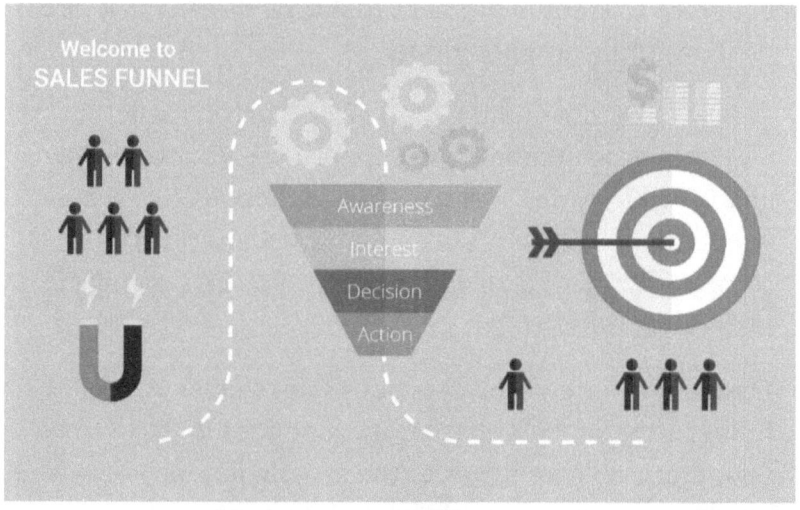

DBAS: Make sure you have KPIs and review them frequently. If not you are just hoping your business is on track.

Turn Data into Cash

Running any business, you want to know how much it costs to acquire a customer and how much value you are extracting per customer. Like the old men's clothing store example, how many people come into the store and how much revenue did that drive.

If you can buy a customer for 25 cents and get 30 cents of revenue out of them, you are creating gross profit. Yet not every customer costs $.25 nor does every customer spend $.30. Breaking down customers into more categories can further reveal where the high margin spots in your business are located.

Value per visit may be different for returning customers versus new ones. Or someone who is searching Google for your brand (your company name) versus someone doing a generic search (like cheap leather wallets) may have wildly different values. The cost of a brand search customer will be the fraction of a cost of a new customer. Because they know who you are and are looking for you specifically. The funnel is narrower. This would mean you should break each of these revenue per user KPIs into two buckets, brand searches and non-brand searches. You could be overpaying in one spot and underpaying in another.

There are tons of tools that help you look at data and some vary from business to business. The most basic tool is a simple spreadsheet like Excel or Google sheets. Here you can automatically calculate formulas that you've created for these KPIs. Excel is a powerful resource that can be used for rudimentary data or to build charts. For data crunching this will cover 90% of what businesses need.

If you want to get complicated with your data, Excel can do that as well. When you decide you want to go to that next level or if you are just interested in the fundamentals, I suggest you get a Lynda.com account. They allow you to watch video tutorials that do an excellent job of teaching techniques from the basic to advanced. This skill will absolutely help you to be a better entrepreneur for your whole career. It's worth investing an hour or two learning how to use Excel properly. This will help you grasp the wide world of analytics and possibly inspire new ways of looking at your data.

Web Based Data Tools

Google Analytics is another tool that can be of significant value in your quest for data superiority. This helps you track customers on your website, the origination source, geographic location, software, platform and many other data points. This service is also free and we love free. (Sometimes I am weary of passing along too much data to Google as they have been known to use it against companies. Same goes for Amazon. This might seem like a tinfoil hat concern, but never hurts to keep your data in as small a circle as possible. But you almost have no choice of using Google initially.)

There is also software that pulls data from a variety of sources and create a web-based dashboard. Cyfe is an example, which brings a bunch of different feeds into one place. They create a visualization of the data and the kpis. This is more advanced and complicated. These are more useful the higher volume you are experiencing. If your site is small stick to simple stuff. As important as data and analytics are don't get too fancy before you need to, it can create analysis paralysis. (This is where you have so much data that you spend all your time looking at the numbers and not actually doing anything.)

Organizing and Comparing Data is Crucial

People have shown me their KPI reports where the report listed info for every day over the last three years. This is more than a thousand points of data for each KPI. It's overwhelming. Organize KPIs in a way that are reasonable and actionable, whether it's month, week etc. Break up the data into multiple tabs on a spreadsheet with one overview tab.

Keep in mind you always want to be able to compare easy to pertinent data points. Maybe the same day this year to the same day last year or this Monday versus last Monday. Control the size in a way that allows you to do this in an orderly fashion or it defeats the purpose of having it.

Don't Be Fooled by Small Samples

When it comes to analytics and making decisions based off analytics be aware of the sample size. If you don't have a large enough sample, it means you haven't seen enough iterations to come to a conclusion. Example of this would be in baseball, a batter got three hits out of four at bats against a certain pitcher. Does this mean the batter will likely get a hit 75% of the time in the future against that pitcher? Probably not. But let's say he faces that pitcher five hundred times and got four hundred hits. You're much more likely to feel comfortable that he's going to do well against that pitcher the next time around. If you have too little data, it's too easy to come to the wrong conclusion.

False Positives and False Negatives

Another pitfall of using data to make decisions is some people make a change but don't give the experiment enough time to see its impact. Let's say you see that on rainy days you think increasing your advertising is a good idea. The next rainy day you turn up your advertising spend and nothing happens. You conclude you were wrong, yet there might have been some other factor that happened that day. Like the stock market was down 500 points and your customer base doesn't spend as much money when the stock market is down. You made a conclusion by using too small a sample size and now think your thesis was invalid. When in fact if you looked at 20 rainy days you would see that you were actually correct. Since you had the false negative you may rule out weather all together as a factor in sales when it in fact does have an impact.

"A Broken Clock is Right Twice a Day"

Don't make a change too quickly or give up on something too fast. Allow enough time for an experiment to play out or you could end up with false positives or false negatives. False positives are usually what people think more about. They think something's working when in reality it is not.

An example from my businesses, I ran two separate travel enterprises, one sold hotels and the other sold vacation packages. We launched the vacation package business and had to factor in the cancellation rate. When we sold purely hotel rooms, we had recorded a cancellation rate of about 10%. These were complicated vacation packages involving vacation ownership (timeshare). Considering they had more moving parts we decided to expect double, a 20% cancellation rate. We opened the business for a few months and reviewed the cancellation rate. It looked like we were accurate as the cancellation rate was about 18%. We didn't really see the boulder falling onto us.

The cancellation rate turned out to be over 40%. These packages followed a completely different timing path than hotel rooms. Tons of people cancelled last minute or just didn't show up at all. Some of this info we didn't receive till 30 days after the trip was supposed to take place. This scenario had created a false positive, we thought we were printing money but turns out our assumed gross profit per customer was way off.

Instead of making money on each transaction, we were losing money on each sale. The opposite of printing money. The false positive came because we weren't patient enough to wait for a full cycle of sales to complete before making conclusions. The window for seeing bookings turn into completed sales was about four months. It took too long to see the error in our ways. The whole time we thought we were building a great business, but we were digging a hole. All because of a small sample size and a false positive.

False Negatives: The Road Almost Taken

False negatives are something that are talked about less but can have equally as damaging impact on your business' development. False negatives are the road not taken, ideas given up on too early. Let's use previous example where you increase your advertising on days where it's raining. The first rainy day doesn't net you increased revenue or profit and you declare this a failure. What you didn't realize is that rainy day sales only increase when the temperature is below 65 degrees. This is because people don't mind the rain when it's warmer.

Now what was a perfectly good and true hypothesis is filed as a bad idea. You don't have unlimited capital so you must make decisions off the smallest amount of data that is possible. Yet experiments have to be thought through beforehand in a way that allows you to collect enough information to make a proper decision.

False positives are harmful because you have now decided that this method does not work and you are unlikely to try it again. If your data was skewed or your experiment contaminated in some way you may end up ignoring an opportunity. This can get even worse, because you inaccurately judged an opportunity, you may be biased against all future versions of this. In our example here where weather plays into sales you may now not be willing to think it has any impact. Yet in truth the temperature outside has a drastic influence on your sales and storm conditions offer massive opportunities for increased margin. But since your first effort failed you have decided to write this off.

DBAS: Don't rush to conclusions without proper data

"Garbage in Garbage out".

Unreliable data creates unreliable conclusions. Double check that you isolate variables as best as possible in experiments. Data exists from lots of different online sources that is just blatantly inaccurate. I've had Google show more conversions than visitors. How can I sell to more people than actually came to my site? Use common sense when looking at data.

The tool you may be employing could be faulty. In this instance analyze the conversion tracker. Get a second opinion by using a second conversion tracker tool to compare the results. Review the numbers of both data sets to determine if the issue is on your side or with the tool. Or if you deem it logical, use an average of the two tools to come closer to accurate metrics.

Be careful that your data has been vetted by isolating it through experiments. Let's say you were being paid for phone calls you are generating from a website. The company paying for the calls gives you a report which says you generated 100 calls in a day. They issued you a unique phone number so your calls aren't comingled with other sources. Yet if this is the only data you have you are forced to rely on their numbers.

"Trust everybody, but always cut the cards"
Benny Binion

Trusting other people's data when significant money is on the line is asking to be cheated. You could get your own phone number and then forward it to the unique number. Then you'd have independent statistics and be able to double check the figures from your customer. If nothing else this will allow you to sleep better at night knowing you aren't being cheated. Sometimes you must be creative to get more than one source of data to allow you to make the correct decisions.

Data is the Chicken and the Egg

Analytics are going to tell you who your customers are but not necessarily who you want them to be. You're going to see the demographics of those coming to your website, store or buying your service and not necessarily seeing the person you want them to be. If for one reason or another, you're only getting in front of suburban housewives, that's who's going to end up buying your product. But if your product would perform best for hipsters in urban areas then your data is not going to reflect that.

Don't be fooled into thinking that who buys your product now is the best audience and only seek to target more of the same. Determining who you want as a customer is a separate track. Avoid letting data control your business. It is a window into what is happening not where you want to go. Mine for new better customers, isolate some data for a different perspective. Say there's a small fraction of customers that are coming from the urban areas, look at their KPIs isolated from all others. How much higher rates do they buy at? How much more money do they spend?

Then you can see if they create a greater value and represent an opportunity.

In this example we are using geography, but this can be applied to other stats easily. You can look at when they buy, the hour of the day, the day of the week. Seasonality is an enormous factor almost every business encounters. (We will get into this in much greater detail later.) Seasonality is something that the web allows you to take great advantage of that brick and mortar cannot.

You can also look at where people buy from, at work or at home? Do they buy on mobile, a desktop, or a tablet? Do they buy via a phone call or maybe they prefer chat? Do they like it in a boat or across a moat? ☺

Breaking down your customer base geographically has become much more accurate. First, we started with area codes and zip codes. Now with IP addresses and mobile phone locations you can hyper target to tiny areas that suit your needs. If your product is for people who have higher income levels, these people usually live in clusters. Use the various geotargeting methods to home in on them.

When I was selling Disney World and Disneyland tickets, people from Arizona are more likely to buy Disneyland tickets than say somebody from Texas. Hence, I'd be willing to pay more for a person who's coming from Arizona than I am from Texas. Not rocket science. Yet as I drilled the data down, I could tell exactly how much more I'd be willing to pay to maintain the target profit margin.

DBAS: The more you know about potential customers the more ways you'll be able to find to get your product in front of them. You will reveal that to yourself through analytics.

The Future of Analytics is Exciting Yet Scary

The future of analytics is big data and A.I. Artificial Intelligence. AI is an automated way of examining numbers for exploitable correlations. Big data is enormous amounts of info that computing power was unable to handle in the past. This allows you to look at the most minute details and compare them across a massive amount records.

AI can create theories and set out to prove them in ways like the ones we have discussed in this chapter. AI notices that if I put umbrellas on my website the day that it rains I'll sell more umbrellas. Next, the AI learns that it's only on days where it's a heavy rain, a light rain we don't really sell umbrellas, it learns as it goes, and it will adjust on the fly. Constantly refining the model. You won't have to make these judgments anymore the AI will make decisions for you.

Kind of scary because they're replacing you, but you must be aware that these methods exist and that it will be part of the future. The better you are at collecting the data and being able to analyze it, the more likely you'll be in a good place to take advantage of something like big data or AI.

Data Sources May Be Bent To Agendas

Data is a balancing act like every other part of your business. You need it to be successful but be weary of the pitfalls. Garbage in Garbage out. False positive and false negatives. Also know certain data companies have an inherent bias and agendas. The largest example is Google, their business has a natural order of things. They want to sell you advertising and manipulate the data to favor you spending more money. You'll find the same true for Facebook. It's an ages old sales method, if you're doing a lot of radio ads they'll show you how good radio advertisements are but billboards suck.

Be on the lookout for that bias. Don't take the data at face value, especially when it's coming from somebody who has a vested interest in where you spend your dollars. Double check how reliable the data is by seeking a second set of figures. Remember there are people out there that will have a bias and that will want to influence the way you look at your data and analytics. This could change the way that you focus your efforts, be your own safety net.

Final Words

Analytics and data are at the core of a successful modern business. Certainly, there are times where you can do it without analytics but those are rare instances. Decide what data you need to collect. Determine what your KPIs will be. Create experiments to improve your business. Make sure you let the experiments run long enough to avoid false positives and negatives. Do your best to navigate the emergence of A.I. and avoid the inherent bias some data companies may have.

The better grasp you have on your data and analyzing it on a daily basis the better chance you will have for a successful business.

Chapter 18: Following and Floating Seasonality

Leveraging seasonality to your advantage is my favorite business hack. This mostly applies to the web-based businesses but can be used to some extent by almost every company.

"A rising tide lifts all boats."

In most businesses there is a moment when demand increases, but capacity can't expand as fast as needed to remain efficient. Imagine if you operated a business that only was open during peak hours. Visualize a coffee shop in a train station, 7:00 a.m. to 9:00 a.m. and 4:00 p.m. to 6:00 p.m. is complete madness. There are lines of customers ready to buy and the staff is moving at top speed. If not for the lines even more people would be buying, but they just can't meet the demand. Now, that's 4 hours out of 24 .

What if you could replicate that for 24 straight hours? You'd have an amazing business. The coffee shop does probably 80 percent of their business in those four hours. That's a boiled down version of seasonality. Look at retailers, most make a disproportionate amount of their money over the Xmas holidays. They can generate as much as 30 to 40 percent of their yearly business during the Christmas season.

Make Every Day a Holiday

How do we locate and understand "seasonality? Demand is going to ebb and flow and the peak windows can be small like a few hours in a coffee shop or large like travel season. Travel is one of my specialties and its season runs from January 15th to August 15th. Yes, people travel the rest of the year, but demand shoots up after the New Year. That's a seven-month window and inside of that time period there are even peaks within the peaks. Smaller windows, you can also look at things like Halloween or Mother's Day. The flower business makes big dollars on Valentine's Day and Mother's Day. Those are their two biggest days of the year, revenue is 20 to 30 times greater than the average day. The goal would be to get in a business that only operated at peak times.

The World Operates 24 Hours a Day.

"Seasonality" can be the hour of the day like the coffee shop example. Look at a call center in the USA. Between midnight and 4:00 a.m. you're not going to get any business. Because in the United States most everyone is asleep. How do you flip this? Time zones. Look at Australia and you will see the hours you are dead in the US perfectly fit for their shopping hours. Pivot and do some of your marketing in Australia during those times.

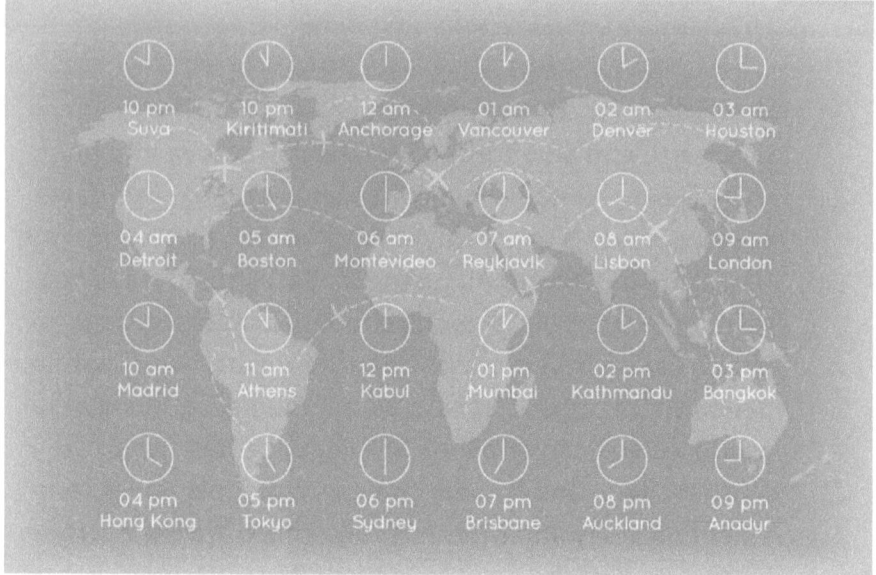

DBAS: The world is a big place. Make that work for you.

Social Media Created Pop Ups

Seasonality wasn't something that could be truly exploited prior to the Internet. The web allows for "pop up businesses". These are businesses that materialize to take advantage of demand and disappear when they are not needed. Whether it be virtual or physical pop-up locations both can take advantage of demand spikes. Examples of the physical version are pop up restaurants or food trucks. They have become popular and more viable because of social media and the Internet.

You couldn't operate a food truck or pop up restaurant at the level you can now without social media. Before you needed the established marketing of saying we're here, we're in one place. You know where to find us when you want us. Instead, now they focus on the product. Which is saying we have great food and we're going to be at this corner at this time or this event on this date. They can promote their product in accordance with where they think there will be demand. A pop-up store can move from one part of the town to another to follow events that bring large groups of people.

Endless Summer

Think of the surfer who chases waves. Attempting to create an endless summer. Imagine a business in which you only focused on high demand times. You sold retail during Christmas, you sold flowers on Valentine's Day and

Mother's Day, you sold Halloween costumes in the month of October, you marketed school supplies in August, and you pushed travel in March. Guess what? You can do exactly that. It's something that I have done. That's a way to create a business that flows to demand.

You may wonder how you can be so nimble and face the competition in each of these industries. When you look at an established business like 1800 Flowers, Expedia or some other seasonal business they're not going to be able to take advantage of all the demand that exists. These companies don't have the infrastructure to properly scale up and down as quickly as you would need to do it. Think of opening a folding table that sold coffee next to that Starbucks in the train station during rush hours. Of course, Starbucks would do way more sales, but your pop up coffee shop would keep cost structure down and suck up the overflow.

The cost to acquire a customer during those time periods will be lower than the rest of the time. The ability to close on a sale is higher. The profitability for that period will be higher than any other. If you can find a way to follow and float seasonality, you're going to find greater profits.

Supplementary Business Model

Maybe the business you're thinking of starting has a natural complimentary business that supplements the income during normal low seasonality. I grew up around the Jersey shore and owners of T-shirt shops on the boardwalk would close during the winter. They would only be open for four months in the summer and then in the colder times they would move down to Florida. Operating in the warmer climate allowed them to follow their customers, tourists.

Another good example of this are landscapers in cold weather parts of the US. Yards are only going to need to be tended to 6-8 months out of the year. For the rest of the time they find cold weather activities that use their equipment and manpower. Like snow removal and hanging Christmas lights. Look closely and you can build revenue sources which are simpatico with each other.

Don't Open a Toy Store the Day After Christmas

Google Will Help You Find Seasonality

You don't want to open your business when peak seasonality just passed . You don't want to open a ski shop the first day of spring as the mountains thaw. Consider this as you're starting to develop the timeline for your business. If you are new to the industry that you are entering and are unaware of the peaks and valleys where do you find the info? If there are publicly traded companies that do what you do, you could listen to their earnings calls or review their income statements for a few years. Their financials would show one quarter larger than all others.

There are simpler ways to find this info, the easiest is Google Trends. This is a tool from Google that allows you to see how many people are searching for a keyword over a set period. You can look over the last day, month, year, or few years. The longer time frame you use, the more precise the data should be.

Also, this tool lets you look at specific geographic regions. Summer in the northern hemisphere is winter in the southern hemisphere. So, if you're selling skis and it's July maybe you should try to market them in South America. This is a helpful tool in finding new ways to manipulate the position of the Earth in relation to the sun to your advantage.

Knowing Seasonality Keeps Your Emotions in Check

A basic part of taking advantage of seasonality is knowing

when these rises and dips in demand will happen. If you don't know the seasonality, you'll be prone to creating panic or celebration unnecessarily. If you open a toy store on Black Friday, the day after Thanksgiving and you thought that the next 30 days were representative of normal sales you would be scaling up your operation and spending money on marketing. But you'll be in for a rude awakening come December 26th.

The flip side of that is true too. One of my favorite sayings is "you don't open a toy store the day after Christmas". If you did you would get a false negative in relation to how sales would be. You'd think the world was ending.

Freaking Out

One of the funnier things in the travel business is the period between Christmas and mid-January. During this time nobody's buying travel because they just spent all their money on holiday gifts. All the travel suppliers freak out. It happens every year. They think there's no business and sales have gone to hell.

In my role as a consultant I'm often taken back by the amount of panic that sets in during this normal predictable dip in sales. Executive teams are in uproar trying to determine what has caused this change in sales and KPIs. They clamor for help coming up with answers. I remind them the cause is just the earth's position to the sun at the current moment. Show them charts of how this has happened like clockwork for years and they still don't want to accept it. They forget every year that they're going to fall off a cliff and don't manage their staffing or cash flow properly.

DBAS: Accept that seasonality exists and plan around it.

Final Words:

Almost every business is seasonal, but to what extent is the question. Some are hyper seasonal like the t shirt shops while others have slight downturns. Being nimble will allow you to take advantage of seasonality. This is a tip and trick to find when demand is escalated. During these times there are heightened levels of profit because of a cheaper cost of customer acquisition and less inefficiency for employees.

Dig into the data, look how seasonality impacts the business you're considering. Also look at businesses that could help bolster your profits when you're out of season. What many people see as a downside to business you can turn into an opportunity to make more money.

Chapter 19: Hack Your Business

Don't be afraid to get under the hood and alter standard operating procedure for your business and think unconventionally. "Think outside the box" is a little too trite.

I prefer the line from the movie The Matrix where Neo asks a child how he bends a spoon with his mind. The child replies:

"Do not try and bend the spoon. That's impossible. Instead, only realize the truth... THERE IS NO SPOON. Then you will see that it not the spoon that bends, it is yourself."

There is no single way to run a business and thinking so is an illusion. You must prod and poke to find new ways to make your business flourish. Find new ways to market, new ways to hire, to gain an edge that will lead to profit and growth.

Let Your Competition Help You

In hacking your business, the goal is to find an exploitable edge over your competitors and the marketplace. Start by looking at how other people in your industry are doing business. There's no reason that you must learn everything on your own. Put the sum power of all others problem solving to your benefit. You can see exactly what your competitors are up to, how they market, where they market, who they market to, who they hire, why they hire, what their organizational structure looks like.

Any information you gather can be put to good use. Get creative. The best information doesn't usually come by entering through the front door. Look at things like LinkedIn profiles of the people that work for the competition. Often individuals will tell you exactly the skills that their company values. There will be insight into organizational structure as well.

Monitor competitor's social media accounts and not just the corporate ones. Follow their top execs or if there is a particular area you are focused on, find those people's accounts. Facebook, Twitter, Instagram. People tend to thump their chest and tell you how smart they are and why. And on their personal accounts they think no one is looking.

Another method is to utilize tools that allow you to reverse engineer their advertising spend. Two that I have used with good success are SEMrush and Spyfu. These will help figure out where they're advertising and how much they're paying.

There are all kinds of intelligence you can learn in a public way. Keep something in mind though just because they're doing it doesn't mean it's right. This is counterintelligence where you try to understand the methods of your competition and find something you have been overlooking. A pot of gold inside of what they're doing that you can replicate.

DBAS: You can't think of everything. Look at what others are doing to show you the way.

Look Around Dummy: Do You Want Fries with That?

Look at other industries and see if you can steal some of their ideas. When I was in college, I recall explaining to my father that I didn't find what I was learning was relevant to becoming an entrepreneur. He told me to go work at McDonald's.

I was a prideful young man and replied, "I'm not going to work at McDonald's. I want to run my own business". His answer was McDonalds is a massive corporation and they figured out how to do a ton of stuff right. Work there for three weeks and you'll learn things about processes and different ways of operating that you can put in your toolbox for the rest of your career. Then quit there and go work at Home Depot, Macy's, Lawn Doctor and so on.

You don't need to work for a company to be inspired by them. Being curious about what tactics have worked for businesses will give you ideas for your own. If you look at successful enterprises , you can hijack what has made them great.

ABH: Always Be Hacking

Take advantage of systems that were built for things other than their intended use. Some of the businesses I have run we were heavy into search engine optimization. Trying to rank number one in Google. There were times that you could absolutely dominate the Google search results. Somebody would type in "Nashville hotels" and we'd have 7 of the top 10 results.

This is because we knew the secret sauce at that moment. As time went by Google got smarter and ranking got harder and harder. But we would reverse engineer it again and again. Using deductive reasoning and examining competitors we were able to understand how to make changes to remain on top.

The way that Google worked then was that if you had links from sites that had a lot of authority (well-known and popular) to your sites, then you would rank high. Getting a popular or big brand site to put a link to yours was difficult and usually happened almost randomly. Instead of bowing to randomness we went out to companies like CNN and The Atlantic asked to buy links on their main page. They were taken aback and would reply "Well we sell advertising. We don't sell links". We would make them offers they couldn't refuse; paying five or ten thousand dollars a month for just a textual link on the main page of CNN.com. This was at a time that these sites were struggling to monetize so they agreed. They didn't understand why this was of value to us, but as long as the checks cashed it was ok. The benefit we gained in Google rankings made the money back 20-fold.

If you determine there is something that you want, but there isn't a market to purchase it, try and create one. The worst thing that could have happened was these companies said no.

Growing up in Atlantic City, New Jersey offered a unique set of circumstances for business hacks. Our family business was operating in this 24-hour town. Far more people were awake at all hours of the day than a normal city. However, the radio stations in the area were run by conglomerates who didn't understand this fact. Overnight ads (from midnight to 6 am) had a lot more value than they did in Des Moines Iowa. The salespeople for the radio companies would throw in these overnight ads almost for free in their proposals. My old man realized that they were undervalued and shifted spend to those times to create greater return on investment. (He called them "dollar a holler" because he'd actually pay $1 a piece for the overnight ads)

There was a time where Google was selling ads on mobile phone search that offered the option to let the customer call you instead of going to your website. Calls have 5x-10x greater value than website clicks, yet they were selling them at the same price. This created a great buying opportunity. Of course, it didn't last, but that's the nature of hacks.

DBAS: Look for spots where universal policy doesn't fit your market and exploit it.

Make Things Work for You

Look at the market and consider using verticals not necessarily for what they are meant. An example is how some event promoters would use StubHub to create awareness. Normally the happenings you find on Stubhub are ones with a lot of interest at large venues with popular performers. Yet promoters putting on concerts or shows with little notoriety found a way to leverage this to their advantage.

Stubhub is meant to be a secondary market, where people who bought tickets can resell them for a profit or because they aren't going to use them. Yet these smart promoters would take their own "house" tickets and put them for sale on StubHub. Not because they were trying to get a premium on tickets but because people now go to StubHub not just to buy tickets but also to look to see what's going on that weekend.

By placing these tickets for sale on Stubhub, it was free advertising for the promoter. It had the added benefit of making it look like the event might be a hot ticket because some people equated being on StubHub with being in demand.

Out of Thin Air

Another hack I have used is where we've created and marketed products that we didn't want to sell. I know that sounds bizarre. Call it bait and switch or sleight of hand, but this isn't immoral or unethical. There are times you can make money from the user in ways other than selling. The product is just window dressing.

An example is where we created a travel club which offered paying members discounts on bookings. Join and get money off the retail price of hotels, flights, attractions and more. The offers we advertised were completely accurate. Yet once the user was on our site, we optimized the experience with revenue from advertising, email marketing and meta searches.

We would charge $100 a year to be a member of the club. Then we would deduct $50 from the price of something for their initial purchase. So, we were actually charging $50 for the club and giving $50 back on your first purchase. This allowed us to advertise lower prices than competitors. Like Disney World tickets for $49.

The club had tremendous value to the user and we originally intended it to be a real product. Yet the data came back showing that it was a tough sale. Yet the user acquisition cost was low and we could produce a profit without selling memberships. We did this through the advertising on the page and other methods. It's a little deceptive, but we weren't cheating or stealing. We just followed the money.

DBAS: The more creative you get with pushing boundaries the more chances you give yourself to be successful.

Be Ready To Be Inspired At Any Time

There are all sorts of things you can do if you use your imagination. Quality domain names- (URLs for websites) got more difficult to come across. Over time all the good ones had been purchased. I would enter hundreds of combinations to try and find one someone missed. What I found is that I would have to take a .net extension or use a hyphen in a word phrase. Dot com domains are still the gold standard and the simpler the title the better.

The business I was in at the time I was using these domains to purchase traffic through different paid advertising options. This was pure arbitrage. Pay $1. Get back $1.20. There was no long-term goal of building brands with the domains. My focus was increasing the R.O.I.

D0NT B3 A SCHMUCK

As an avid online poker and video game player, I noticed that when people would make their screen names (their online identity) that they'd often replace the O with a 0 (zero) the E with a 3. They did this because somebody had already taken the handle that they wanted. Seemed like a simple hack and I was inspired to see if I could use it on my business. Let me buy some domains with these tactics.

Right away it was evident that if I put a zero in place of the letter O I could buy amazing domains. Major city names like Orland0.com, NewY0rkcity.com, and SanDieg0 were all available. These were terrible branding domains, but for hacking the landscape of online advertising they were perfect. The real counterpart domains using the traditional letters were undeveloped. So, I wasn't hijacking anyone's brand.

People didn't recognize the difference when looking at an ad and would click on mine at much higher rates than before. This brought my cost lower while revenue stayed the same. Turned out to be a great return just by willing to be inspired while playing poker.

Inspiration can be found everywhere. Read publications or blogs that relate to what you do. This will be a looking glass into what the market is doing. Seeing how people do things in any corner of the world can be applied to your business. Keep an open mind and let your imagination run wild.

Final Words: Hack your business. Take advantage of systems that weren't necessarily built for what you use them for. Stay up to date on your industry and your competitors. Read Read Read. Find any way you can to be inspired, to get under the hood and look at things differently. Hack your business continually because it's the quickest way to succeed.

Chapter 20: Build a Network

Build a network. It's important to expand your circle when you start a new business. Create and foster positive lasting relationships wherever you can.

A great podcast for the entertainment industry is by a guy named of Barry Katz. In every episode, while he's interviewing famous people behind the scenes or in front of the camera, he repeats the mantra "relationships, remember people, relationships".

He is showing that you'll find this theme repeatedly. People who are successful have seeded relationships. Kept them alive and going for many years. You never know when the relationships you started years ago will come to help you out today.

"It's not just what you know, it's who you know."

That's an old saying but it's still true in the modern world. Think about that as you're growing your business. When it comes to networking consider that you want to meet people so that you can foster better relationships. Terms with vendors, when you sell your company, raise capital or whatever it will be easier with good relationships.

Networks are educational, people give you info about your business or the experiences they've had which will save you time and money. That's just as important as the ability to make a deal. Now, where do you start growing your circle to help your business?

The People You Know and Know You.

Get in touch with former colleagues, friends, and family whoever it may be. Just say hi. You've possibly hit some of these people up to raise money. If you haven't, it's time to inform them of your business and to speak the narrative of your company. This way they can understand who you are now and what you do. If you know where you're lacking, or you know where you're trying to go you can pass this info on to them during your conversations.

These are people who know your skills or your work. They are more likely to recommend you or put you in a good position to find ways to grow your business. People like helping people.

Conventions and Conferences

Attend conventions and conferences, these are the supermarkets of networking. The shelves are stocked with people to meet and often they are there for the same reason. Conferences and conventions do differ. Conventions are usually tradeshows where people are setting up booths to sell perspective clients. Conferences are more of a learning forum. Both offer unique opportunities to expand your network.

The downside of attending these events is they can be expensive. Not only the cost of the entrance, but there is usually travel involved.

DBAS: Go to conferences near you. It saves money.

At these events set a goal to get one concrete benefit out of each convention or conference. This could be a tactic, a connection, or whatever. But that one core asset can pay for the cost of the conference if you apply it across your business.

[This isn't about the networks but it's a way to defer the costs of conventions. If you learn a single thing that makes your business grow 1 percent, a convention will pay for itself. That leaves you free to network without feeling the burden of the expense. I keep a note pad for each individual event I attend to memorialize the inspirational ideas. I have never failed to gain that nugget that pushed my business forward at least 1%.

TANGENT

Giving it All Away

Conferences are education seminars with a few exhibitor booths thrown in too. At these events, don't just look at the topics of the seminars, but what position the people presenting have in their company. In these panels or seminars people will share information that they shouldn't. They give away some of their secret sauce.

This is human nature, if you stand in front of an audience you want to show them how smart you are. Ego or insecurity gets the best of them. Often unknowingly they'll give you gifts that will keep on giving. You will be surprised how people divulge this info. Outside of ego, what happens is that the knowledge is so engrained in them that they pass it to you without a second thought. (So very nice of them. LOL)

Get Down With the Q&A

Usually there'll be a question and answer period after the presentations. This is a great opportunity for you to take advantage, for two reasons. Number one is you get an  expert opinion on a topic related to your business. Second, your voice will be heard, your face will be seen by the other people attending the convention. A way to advertise yourself to other attendees and create that network. So as you're walking down the hall after some symposium somebody may stop you and say oh I heard you talking about such and such. And that's an issue for me also.

Or they might have a solution to your problem "What I found is this and that or maybe we should get together and talk about this and have a drink later afterwards" Conventions are a target rich environment for networking hence don't ignore them. There will be information there that you won't have access to elsewhere.

Step Outside Your Bubble

The world is smaller because of the Internet and social media but being immersed in a topic by attending an event can help you in ways you might not have considered. Once you have hit the conventions and conferences for your own industry, venture out. People get myopic and tune out what is happening in the rest of the world. Go to more general conventions to get inspiration.

For a while, the Consumer Electronics Show in Las Vegas was my method of seeing the world better. I wasn't a hardware producer or a vendor for any of the products featured there. Yet seeing the emerging technologies allowed my imagination to run wild. Additionally, I could find people that were going to be on the next frontiers of business. Attending CES got me first shot to create relationships early on with companies.

People who are pushing new products are much more open to hearing and listening than established ones. Their relationships are not yet defined so they are naturally open to talk to anyone. Burgeoning companies were where I focused my time. Laying the groundwork for a time when these firms would become part of the mainstream landscape.

Another conference I found to be helpful was E3, which is the largest expo for video games in the United States. My curiosity about virtual reality and working in that space was what pushed me in this direction. The newest demos of VR software and hardware were in one place. What I was only able to read about or get piece meal was under one roof. Making it a great place to learn, be inspired or to have your voice heard.

The pioneers of products were accessible and open to the idea of working with anyone who was headed in the same direction. There is no virtual way to build this type of connection and hence an amazing way to grow your network.

These events will expand your circle. You never know when the phone is going to ring or you get an e-mail from a person you met during one of these conventions. These types of connections can alter your company's future.

DBAS: Don't get stuck in the bubble of your industry 24/7. You will begin to think like the herd and that isn't going to help you get where you want.

Social Media Networking

Before social media it was difficult to grow your network from a distance. Now Twitter, Facebook and LinkedIn have all made it much easier for you to connect with people in your industry. Potential vendors, consumers, collaborators are all within a few mouse clicks.

Creating a unique point of view for your online persona can be helpful in making you stand out from others. Instigate dialogue by commenting or reacting to things going on in your industry or that relate to your business. The goal is to get a conversation going on a social platform that will get your face in front of people that you're interested in connecting with. The hardest part of getting to work with someone is breaking down that initial wall. Getting them to a position that they are open to hearing your point of view is a big step.

Interacting with partners and supplies are some of the most valuable places for networking on social media. That initial wall has been broken and you can use these platforms to cement your relationships. Competitors are less likely to engage with you. Better to follow them so you can see what they're thinking, what's going through their brain at any given moment. It's almost a window to the soul.

227

Online relationships can grow quite solid, but they often take longer than it would in the physical form. Over the years I have made many friends all over the world through social media. Most of whom I've never met. As much as hand-to-hand contact can't be replaced in this world, there is volume that you can get through social media.

Unfortunately, it is degrading into a numbers game. Social media spam has become the norm. Because you can try to talk to companies in different countries and places this is being gamed. If I were going to utilize the throw shit against the wall method on social media, I would separate my own personal account from my company.

DBAS: You carry your name with you for the rest of your life, companies come and go.

Side Tracked: Don't Burn Bridges

Try not to burn bridges for the sake of burning bridges. Social media invites conflict. Avoid engaging in any Twitter or Facebook battles with people in your industry. No matter how much of a firebrand or headstrong person you may be. It's OK to speak your opinion but remember the goal is to create a circle and not to cut people off.

Meetups: Don't Be Afraid of People

Another way to expand your circle are Meetups (meetup.com) which is a great site for startups. Most likely there'll be groups that relate directly to your industry which you can join. They hold physical and virtual meetings/events regularly, where you can get to meet likeminded individuals.   If no groups exist, you can start a meet up in your area. You become the thought leader and see who's around you. Either path is a quick way to build your local network. A method to find potential employees or partners for the future.

Like conventions or conferences consider going beyond your specific industry. Maybe there are groups where people who are going through the same things as you. For instance, most cities have meetups for startups.

Beyond business there are a lot of hobbyists holding meetups. I mentioned virtual reality before and at the beginning the field was made up of mostly hobbyists. VR wasn't about the commercialization of the product. During this phase, meetups allowed me to talk to people who were enthusiastic and imaginative but had little interest in the business side. A unique perspective that couldn't be found elsewhere.

Creating networks is about interacting with new people who are doing things or know info that you don't. Meetups are full of both of those. They combine the physical and social media worlds. Creating possibilities of connections that can evolve and turn into more friends or compatriots.

DBAS: Go to a meetup, Netflix will be there when you get home.

Vendors/Suppliers are Future Partners

Consider the status of your relationships with people who work at your vendors and suppliers. By creating personal relationships with these people, you can reap many benefits. There are short term rewards. Like I've found collecting money is a lot easier from somebody whom with you have a personal bond. You can solve problems faster if you know them. Call and talk through a problem instead of a stringent back and forth in email. This is because you can utilize emotions like guilt and loyalty to help get your desired result. Additionally, you are likely to get intel on your suppliers. Better pricing. Knowledge of mergers and acquisitions. Friends gossip. It is human nature.

Vendors are also a great place to find potential employees. When you want to be more vertically integrated these people already have a working knowledge of how your company operates. An example is my first C.T.O. I recruited because he was running our hosting and web access for a third party. After time we got to talking and felt like it would be a good fit. That's an efficient way to grow your business.

Suppliers or partners are often the companies who will attempt to acquire you. Big companies look to grow through acquiring strong partners. They get a good sense that you're a decent human being, a good businessperson and growing a valuable asset. Having that personal relationship makes them more open to the idea of bringing you into the fold. That's where these relationships can bring heavy rewards.

Simple Tip: Little Tokens Go A Long Way

Doing something simple but showing thoughtfulness will magnify the bond of your relationships. Send friends/suppliers/partners holiday gifts or cards. This is not about doing something extravagant but showing that you care. Furthering this personal relationship.

There are people out there that could not care less about these tokens and they goes in the trash. Yet to most people this means something, and it will strengthen your bond. People like to be acknowledged. Even those who threw it in the trash like it on some crazy power-hungry level. Either way it will benefit to you.

Side Note: This is not just about the financial benefit of growing your company. Being connected to human beings and your business will make the journey more enriching for you.

General Organizations

These are a bit antiquated, but we want to expand our network any way we can. Chamber of Commerce, political organizations, charities etc. These make it easy for you to get amongst people of differing levels of wealth, ethnic backgrounds, ages, experience, or education. Exposing you to things that may be going on outside of your daily life.

I don't want to undersell the value of being involved in charitable causes. Yet I prefer to look more at those for the value of making you a more enlightened person than growing your business. But all roads lead to Rome.

Final Words:

Expanding your circle is opening yourself up to opportunity. Try to do it daily. Parties, conventions, conferences, social media, meetups and almost any gathering of people. If there are projects that are near and dear to your heart you show people passion. They will look to be engaged with you because they'll see you in a positive light. Ultimately, you've got to roll up your sleeves and find more people to be connected to and treat them in a way that you want to be treated.

Get out there and as Barry Katz says "relationships, everybody relationships"

Chapter 21: Putting Your Money Where Your Month Is

One of the hardest things in business is getting the ball moving. A way to fast track this is by being willing to prove yourself to customers. Be eager to put your time, energy and skills into projects for less than market value. Often you must do it for free. This sucks, I know, but breaking down that first door is the hardest. If you're confident in what you do, then you can offer your skills a discount/free and hope you get return. This method immediately builds trust with any potential client.

There are a few ways to go about this that we will explore in this chapter. Offering your service or product free is an obvious one. Asking for no upfront money is another option. Here you only get paid if the customer is satisfied with the result. The type of product or service you are selling will dictate some of this. Each method requires a different approach and they do have some downsides.

There's No Such Thing as a Free Lunch?

Giving away something for free should be the easiest path to getting customers. If they won't take your services or products with no cost that's a big red flag. Once you do find people to take you up on the free sample think through the process of converting them to a paying customer.

You usually offer something for free when the margins are high, and the cost associated with giving it for free is low. For example, if you run a site that gives expert advice on the stock market, offering a free trial to a customer won't cost you much of anything. The value of a subscriber over the lifetime of their use could be $100s or $1,000s. If you retain just a small portion of the free trials you will have a great business. Ask yourself if there is something you can giveaway to introduce yourself to customers.

The downside other than not getting paid is that offering something for free can devalue your product. If people get it for free, then it can be difficult mentally for them to turn around and pay for it.

Only If It Works

You can craft offers with no upfront payment. This is obviously harder than free as you are letting the potential customer know that they may have to be out of pocket. This tactic can backfire if you try to sell it improperly and come across like a used car salesman. You should be trying to get this person interested in one of your paid programs. But relent and offer a no money up front package when the rest doesn't look like it will happen.

I'm a big fan of these types of offers because they allow you to set goals for working with a client right out of the gate. You are telling them what you plan on achieving and they are accepting this as valuable. If you hit these goals, you will create long term loyalty.

These programs take some creativity and sales savvy to get into place. If you approach a potential customer and say, "I'll do it with no risk to you. If you don't like the results don't pay me". That may not give you the opportunity, believe it or not. People are still going to have to invest the time to talk to you, look at the results and measure the value. Most businesspeople need a buy in emotionally even if they are getting something for free or at no risk. Often you can use these types of offers to get a client who is on the fence.

DBAS: Get people to try your product. Even if you have to make an abnormal deal.

When I was in high school and college, I had taken over a business running a local tourist newspaper.

One of my mentors had been running a bunch of these papers all over New Jersey. He was an entrepreneur with a ton of experience, and I was just 17 years old. He knew me since I was a child, my father had advertised in one of his papers over the years. I guess he saw that twinkle in my eye and offered me an opportunity. He handed over the reins for running a newspaper for Ocean

City, New Jersey. I'd never done anything like this, but that never stopped me before or since.

I must admit I was intimidated at first. How was I going to get these grizzled adults to buy ad space in my newspaper? I had zero technique. My mentor took me out on a training session. In a few short hours he showed me how to sell advertising. The one tactic that he used that I gravitated to immediately was the performance approach.

He'd go into a perspective business and say "let's put a coupon in the ad and you tell me how many coupons you need to get to make the ad worthwhile. You need to get 20 in a week. Ok I'll come back in a week and we'll count the coupons. You have 20 coupons you pay. You don't have 20 coupons you don't pay. It's FREE. "

He was willing to put his money where my mouth was. That was my first experience with the prove it mentality. The strategy works well in advertising because it's hard for the person on the other side of the table to argue against. If you come across as honest and authentic most people will give you a shot. You are showing confidence in your product and a desire to help their business. (Also, you are displaying belief in their business. That people will want what they are selling.)

What is Your Coupon?

 This is a tactic that I've employed throughout my entire career and I highly recommend you figure out how it applies to your business. What is your coupon? What is your thing that you can offer and track? This will help you grow your business.

Part of the "coupon" strategy is that you must have clear goals when you try a free or no upfront money offer. This is the key to any deal, but even more so when you only win if you perform. Always make sure that the goals are clear going into a deal with a new client or you are setting yourself up for failure.

Coupons are a bit outdated even though there are a ton of offer sites on the Internet. On the web you can track conversions. If someone gives you a special offer to advertise for them, it would be easy to see if you were able to succeed. The coupon is just a term for a measurable action that will make your customer feel like you have succeeded. The internet with its endless statistics doesn't eliminate this concept, it expands it. If your customer knows their data, they can easily pass along to you a way you can prove success.

Sidetracked : Money Back Guarantee

Another method you can try is the money back guarantee. If the customer doesn't like the product, they can return it within a set period of time for a full refund, no questions asked. This creates a level of confidence in your product and usually won't hurt you. This is done in retail situations of high margin like vitamins, supplements, mattresses. The return amount is factored into your overall cost of goods sold. This method is effective because people are usually too lazy to return something even if they don't like it.

Setting Up the Conversion

During the first meeting where you make the offer you should always ask for a promise of a follow up discussion. One where you will have the opportunity to pitch them on the results and turn them into a paying client. Be clear about this with the potential client during the low impact sale.

An example is a company that has a tool that analyzes data for your business. This tool looks at your security tapes for 30 days and counts how many people come into the building. Then it checks how many go to the cash register. The company offers to give the service away for 30 days. After that they are going to come back with the data to talk over the results. Without the follow up meeting there is no way to show that what they did has value.

Clear Goals

Having goals clearly stated will codify what is success for you in this project. You can immediately start working towards these mile markers instead of playing guessing games on what a customer wants. In the instance where the customer wanted to get coupons (to prove people were being moved by the advertisement), I made sure that I placed their ad on a lower right-hand corner of the page. This is the page position where somebody is more likely to cut out a coupon. Because I knew what success was, I could plot my action steps accordingly. Having those clear goals will let you know whether you're doing your job right.

Important Tip: Ask for a testimonial from someone whom you've given a free shot. Have them give you a quote about their experience. Or you can ask for data to share in future promotions.

Bet the If Come

A tactic which is a branch of the no money down concept is called the "if Come". This is an approach where if you hit a specified target it will trigger an action by the client. Free offers with no strings attached are appropriate sometimes and if come work better for other. If possible, try for the if come because it doesn't devalue your product. It forces you to produce. The coupon example from earlier is an if come. If we get you 20 coupons then you will pay us for the advertising.

When crafting a prove it offer you should look at your product structure and target customers. As I mentioned earlier, these tactics are best for high margin environments. They don't work that well if you have a limited amount of product unless if it will expire like ad space or a hotel room. If the time passes and these products aren't used, they end up having zero value.

These deals are meant to create repeat customers not one-time sales. You're trying to put your product in the hands of someone who hasn't used it yet but could use it over and over.

SideTracked **Again:** There are some group promotions that you could participate in to do a prove it model. An example would be a fixed price meal offering for a restaurant. Many cities across the US pick a slow week in the restaurant business and do special offers across dozens of locations. "Restaurant Week" Something like $20 for a full meal at any restaurant participating. This is a prove it offer in the sense that you are selling your goods at less than standard price in hopes of the diners returning at a later date. You also get the added benefit of being part of any advertising that goes along with promoting the event. Prove it offers come in many forms.

People Actually Want You to Succeed

Something to keep in mind when you're doing the prove it deals, people don't want you to work for free. That's an overlooked part about these tactics. Once they've committed to working with you, if you show them reasonable performance, they will likely find a way to be fair with you.

During your follow up meeting with the client, you may ask for $2,000 for the service you provided already. They don't want to take advantage, so they'll let you know it's only worth $1,000 to them. That $1,000 for your service might be profitable and worthy of continuing. Or they will feel guilty and give you a try a second time around because they know they didn't have to pay full price initially.

The results of prove it offers will give you a better sense of whether your product is succeeding or failing. If you come back to a client to "count coupons" and they had four but were expecting a hundred you know your value proposition isn't working. You are not to going to bark up that tree anymore.

You do have to assess whether you think they're keeping proper accounting and creating reliable data. If not that can muddy the process. There is a certain amount of trust involved in prove it offers. If you don't have any trust in the client, it might be best to just move along. Decent people want you to be successful. They want to find somebody who does something of value for them.

Prove It to Improve It

Employing these tactics, you'll be able to price your products better. If you determine that if you put somebody on the back cover of the magazine, they get a thousand coupons you know you can charge a lot more. Also, you can compare your own products to one another. If one performs 10 times better than another you can price them accordingly. Also, knowing what your product is worth helps you be able to assess how viable your business is at present. If you aren't offering enough value to make a profit you will have to get back in the lab and improve your product.

If you were to choose the hardline sales approach of not employing prove it offers you likely will sell considerably less. Even if the profit were the same between the two approaches, with standard sales approach you lost the opportunity to fine tune your product.

If you wait for somebody to pay you full price upfront, you may not have had the ability to tweak your product to make it better. You could be undercharging with prove it offers, but you'll learn and be able to increase your prices accordingly. Getting in the repetitions of serving customers early on has benefits that magnify as your business grows.

DBAS: The higher level of belief you have in your product the easier it will be to sell.

Revenue Sharing: Affiliate & Partner Up

Another prove it tactic is doing revenue sharing or profit sharing deals. These are arrangements where you get a piece of sales or profit from the project. This way the person you are working with only pays you for performance. This is similar to a company hiring a commission only salesperson. If you believe you will create increased sales or profit for a company agree to a deal that will pay you a portion of the increases.

Create Leverage for New Deals

Another benefit of doing prove it deals is you can build a portfolio, which can create leverage. A client will be more likely to give you a chance once they know you work with their competition. I used this tactic on restaurants when selling advertising as a college kid. There were two seafood restaurants open on one street. I gave one of them a free trial then waited till the magazine came out and then visited the competition. I'd say, "How would you like to advertise? Your competitions got a full page." It doesn't matter whether the first guy paid for it or not. The second guy has no idea the first guy got it for free. Now it's much easier to sell because it's a monkey see monkey do world.

You can also surf off the brands of the people you give free trials. (Surfing brands is a big deal and will get more into it next chapter). Just being related to a big-name client in an industry or in a geographic area may carry weight. These types of deals help build a network and get your name out.

Let's say you are in the IT support business, you could offer the largest TV station a free trial. Then when you go out to sell others, you could easily drop in that you do tech support for ABC 7. Leverage the people who you give prove it deals. Leverage every little edge you can. Little advantages will add up to a winning strategy.

Sidetracked: Give it away now.

Previously I mentioned you may end up with expiring inventory like advertising, food, tickets or hotel rooms. Where the next day they are going to be valueless. Or even your own time, where you have a free afternoon to do some work for someone. If you have expiring assets, consider giving them away with no immediate idea of the return. This is done in an attempt to grow goodwill. People like to feel important and getting free stuff does just that. You might be taking a total loss today, but you may be gaining the asset of a relationship down the road.

Trade Your Way in the Door

Your goal often is to get in the door and show a client how well you perform. Bartering services or products for theirs is about as old a tactic as there is. This does seem like something from a century ago but there are still businesses that are willing to do trade. These are usually other companies that have high margins. (Sound familiar?) Also you need to focus on businesses that have a simple hierarchy, where you can speak directly to a decision maker.

Simple example: If you need some furniture and you operate a cleaning company, go to the furniture store. Walk around, find the manager and tell them "it looks like you could benefit from a high-quality cleaning to make your product and showroom sparkle. How would you like to have somebody come in here and clean it for a full day? Normally that would be $1,000 but I'll do it for a few desks." They might just say yes.

They're willing to trade because furniture stores can be operating on 200-300% markup. What do you care? If you were going to have to go in your pocket to spend a $1,000 on desks, but instead you now pay $400 worth of labor to clean the furniture store. Everybody wins. Not only have you made a theoretical profit, but you now have a potential recurring client. Someone who has seen how well you perform. Any way to get in the door and show your stuff is a win.

Final Words

Be creative about finding ways to prove yourself. Every one of these deals is an opportunity to grow your business. To learn about and refine your company. Getting in repetitions will let you get further faster. Too many people feel like everything must be perfect for that first client or that first move. Nothing is going to replace the experience you get by actually doing something. The hardest thing to do is establish a relationship with a customer or a client. Use any means necessary to make this happen.

DBAS: Sit down and brainstorm some prove it deals for your company.

Chapter 22: Surfing Brands... The Fast Lane to Profit

This concept has made me more money than any other in this book. In actuality it probably should be a book of its own. This chapter is not about what you should do to build your brand, or what your brand should be, that is a greater existential question. My goal here is to show you how to take other people's brands and leverage them to build your business.

Brands are omnipresent in today's consumer environment. Clothes, beverages, cold medicine, cars, computers. There isn't any established industry that doesn't have brands that their consumers recognize. Brands are extremely valuable and hence they're expensive or time consuming to build. Although brands aren't a new concept their pervasiveness continues to grow each year. If you look at pictures from the 60s and 70s almost no clothes had logos on them. Nowadays people wear their brand loyalty literally on their chest, like it was a crest of their family.

Brands Create an Instant Feeling

 Brands are meant to create an emotion in people. Know what action you want your customers to take and then you can leverage other brands to help

247

produce the emotion to act. Examples of this would be credibility, desire, excitement, anger, hip/trendy, secure or safe. Brands produce one or more of these emotions in a potential customer or client. Create a list of brands that mirror the emotions you are looking for in your industry or tangential industries.

Are there brands that people associate with your products and services? Many big brands are spending mega dollars making people understand who they are and what they do. By latching onto someone else's brand it cuts the amount of teaching you have to do to a new customer. Aligning your brand with existing ones is almost always cheaper and faster than trying to go it alone.

Side Note: Brand marketing channels for online companies are usually the cheapest. Meaning people who already know the brand and are looking for that specific brand have the lowest customer acquisition cost.

Cutting Them Off at the Pass

Marketing your products to people who are already looking for known brands lets pick off customers at a critical point. Let's say you want to sell an off-brand or an emerging brand products/services. The most cost-effective way to do this is associate with a known brand product. Then show the benefits of buying your product versus the known one.

If you know you wanted to sell somebody a microwave from an off brand you find a GE or Samsung product. Show the customer, here's the microwave you know and here's our brand. By showing the brand they know you have created credibility for yours just by being next to it. Then you can get to your sales pitch "this is why ours is just as good, but it costs less money and you should buy from us." Simple straight forward.

DBAS: People who are ready to buy immediately are the most profitable customers.

Hijack Their Brand

In the world of marketing on the Internet you target the keywords of a brand that you think you can surf. In the example above, you would buy keywords like "GE microwaves".

You may have a product catalog of thousands of items all from different brands. It is cheaper to market 'Ralph Lauren Polo Shirt' than it is just 'Polo Shirt'. You are attempting to hijack the customer when they are near the end of the buying funnel. The closer a customer is to buying the more valuable they become.

If you look at the graphic of the online buying funnel you are getting to the customer at the finalist stage. This is right before they buy. This customer could cost 80% less

than at the potential stage and make 300% more revenue. That's why brand hijacking is so profitable.

Brands aren't that fond of people surfing them and sometimes it requires their express permission. There are legal gymnastics you can do to circumvent this but it's up to you to try to decide your acceptable level of risk. The reason brands fight against these tactics is because of their effectiveness. This allows competitors to get cheaper marketing which has been subsidized by the known brand.

Are You a Member?

Brands aren't just products they can be organizations. Think about if you are a member of an industry organization that would bring you credibility. Something like the Better Business Bureau. You could utilize their logo to leverage their brand to make you seem more credible or worthwhile. Just look at that BBB logo. You immediately think better of the page you are reading. Human emotions are dumb and exploitable.

Integrity   Trust   Reliable   Authentic   Reputation   Regard   Commitment

What Brands Do You Use?

Brands can also be items that are used during the process of creating or delivering your product. These services would bring you credibility, like security software on a website. A graphic or logo on your website where you can let people know that it's a secure process. If it's been scanned by Norton Antivirus or whomever, use those logos and it'll make people feel safe and secure.

Another example would be if you go to a restaurant and they say we use USDA prime beef or KOBE beef. They are using the brands of the ingredients in their food to make the customer emote quality. Think about what brands you use to make your product. You can surf those brands to heighten perception of your product.

Leverage Brand of Review Sites

Reviews have become a cornerstone of purchasing and decision making. A Yelp review is more powerful than a random testimonial. The bigger the brand that houses the review, the more credible the review becomes. If you've ever watched a trailer for a movie there will be reviews that flash across the screen and says "The best movie of the year" If the review comes from Joe Blow's newspaper in a small town in Kansas it's not going to have the impact as if the review was from The New York Times.

If you watch, the more important the publication is, the bigger the font they use to show the source of the review. If they write it small, then you know it's probably a load of bullshit from a source you never heard of.

Get reviews on major platforms like Yelp or Amazon. Then leverage their brand by displaying those reviews on your site with their logos.

DBAS: Get friends and family to review your service. Seeding good reviews goes a long way.

Backdoor Public Relations Surfing

Public Relations is a solid way to surf big brands to get free advertising for your company. You can set a trap for media sources by creating brand intersecting PR. You do this by making press releases that include your partners with big brands. Specifically, so you can grab attention from those journalists who cover them. I've done this with Hotels.com and other publicly traded companies. We would launch a new product and part of the new offering utilized a major brand, we would list their name and stock exchange ticker symbol on the press release.

This was always done with the consent of the partner, but usually through back channels and not through their PR departments (who likely would have seen through the move). If you do have an intimate relationship with a publicly traded company and you can do a press release that includes them it's going to bring you credibility and exposure. This tactic will create buzz around what you're doing and will cost next to nothing.

Leveraging Media Coverage by Brands

When it comes to media obviously the platforms with the widest reach are opportunities to leverage a brand. By getting media coverage you can use this on your site or presentations to increase your credibility. Saying "as seen in the New York Times" or as "seen on CNN" is a tried and true tactic. If you get a chance to be interviewed by a news outlet or any media company, you can always use it to make your brand more attractive.

Every Bit Helps. Surf Small Waves Too.

Smaller brands can also have value in leveraging. Usually these are for more niche goals. Speaking at high profile events or conferences will allow you to use their brand as tacit validation. Go on podcasts, radio shows. Each of these has a brand and to their loyal following appearing on these shows like it or not is a seal of approval.

Trojan Horse of Cross Promotion – Circular Branding

The last method of brand surfing I'll discuss is where you have other companies surf your brand. Circular logic I know, but it's called cross promoting. Is there a way to get your customers or vendors to promote your product? Just like you use companies to build your credibility, by letting others use your brand to promote them it makes your brand more credible. There are a million variations of this concept like Coke putting their name on fridges that house beverages at restaurants. There are surely versions of this method that will fit your business.

Final Words:

Now you know the secret of surfing other people's brands to sell product, increase credibility, cut marketing costs, and gain media exposure. This is a tool that many underutilize. If you want to sell microwaves, it is much easier to ride in the wake of brand names like Samsung or Whirlpool etc. People are going to be looking for names that they know. They're not looking for Joe's microwave shop on the Internet. By leveraging the brands of the products that people have spent years developing you create an emotion that allows you to cut costs or increase sales. Skip all the expensive customer education by tapping into existing emotions.

DBAS: Surf other people's brands. This is a great shortcut to profit.

Chapter 23: What If You Get Hit By a Bus?

You can be too important to your company. I know that's hard to believe. You're powerful and have strengths and skills of ten different people. Being excellent at one thing most likely won't be enough when you start your company. To succeed as a startup, you are going to have to be great at a variety of tasks and play many roles. However, as the company grows you need to build an organization that isn't entirely on your shoulders. If not, this will stunt the growth of your company and have other downsides you might not expect.

Hit by a Bus

Here's a scenario that helps you look at your business without you. What if you got hit by a bus tomorrow? What would happen to your company?

People use this hypothetical because it's an easy way of creating a situation where you are gone without using the more likely events which would cause you to not be there. Like if you have family problems, health issues, got bored of the business, went crazy, whatever it may be. So, what if you got hit by a bus? If the answer is that the company would likely fold, that's a problem.

We've talked about selling your company before and if you're irreplaceable, potential buyers will be afraid of the value of the company without you. They don't really know how to assess what the company's worth without you in it. If you are disproportionately important to the company's future, they must ensure you will stay on after a sale. Even then it will be hard to know whether they can keep you motivated if you agree to stay. It's nice for the ego to think the company would collapse without you, but it's bad for the wallet and likely your heart.

Chained to Your Desk

If you're indispensable and irreplaceable you won't be able to go on vacation. Yet you need to unplug and recharge to be at the height of your powers. If things fall to shit while you're gone it'll be hard for you to relax. Some people have the illusion that things crumble when they are absent. They almost need it to happen because it helps feed their egomania.

If you can't unplug, you're going to burn out. The weight will always land on you no matter how much you love what you're doing. Being indispensable will take a toll on different parts of your life physical, social, romantic, family. Whatever you can think of, it will wear it down. Put effort into making sure this doesn't happen.

DBAS: A great business isn't one that needs you 24/7.

Build an Organization

How do you avoid being too important? You can't clone yourself, so the only choice you have is to build an organization.

Hopefully you've hired great people. The easiest way to allow yourself to not be bigger than the team is to build a strong organization around you. People who run their corners of the company like a Swiss watch. If this is the case, you can slowly change your job from wearing 10 hats to pointing the direction of the company going forward. This is a role you don't have to do 24 hours a day 7 days a week. Make this shift from the center of the universe to the captain who is steering the ship.

Hierarchy Is Necessary

Creating a clear hierarchy is part of avoiding problems with being indispensable. People must know who's responsible for what and how information flows. If everything runs through you, you're just a giant octopus with your hands in everything. You're the hub for all information and your capacity to manage all the data flow can limit growth. Also, it will be harder to function smoothly if you are out of the equation. If you create a hierarchy where you are counting on your core staff directly to relay information regularly, you free up people to work and not have to wait on you.

If the tech department and marketing department are

working on a project not every piece of info must run across your desk. There is a limit to what one person can do. Trust the people under you to perform. This doesn't mean that you don't spot check their work or cut out communication with everyone underneath them in the hierarchy. The goal is that on a standard day the team can operate without your nod of approval on every little thing. Train your team to know the difference between big decisions and little ones. Thus, they know when your input is necessary.

Test it With Training Wheels

The only way to know if your company could handle you getting hit by a bus is to take a hiatus of some kind. By taking breaks you will allow yourself to test the systems you have put into place. This doesn't mean you have to disappear to the South of France for a month. Start by turning off your phone while going away for a day or two. See what happens. You can always have a failsafe plan if the world is on fire. A method how somebody can get in touch with you in case of emergency.

In this modern age people are too connected and it has dual consequences. People can't unplug which burns them out faster. Also, you are never disconnected so you end up building an organization which is not on sound footing. One that can implode without an individual. Try to disconnect for a short period and it will help you avoid this trouble.

Final Words:

You must be indispensable to your business at first. The company is too small to not count on you. As it grows, you must build an organization that is capable of surviving without you. Cast your ego aside because if you don't, you will limit your lifestyle, ceiling and exits.

Chapter 24: Momentum and Gotchas

Momentum and gotcha's two things that business people don't think about before starting their journey.

Momentum "the big mo", that's the good feeling when you're executing your plan and moving forward with ease. People take momentum for granted once they have achieved it, but you must guard it delicately. Be on the lookout for things that will hinder momentum and derail your progress. Remember it's much easier to move forward once things are headed in the right direction.

Newton's First Law of Motion states that a body at rest will remain at rest unless an outside force acts on it, and a body in motion at a constant velocity will remain in motion in a straight line unless acted upon by an outside force.

You will get derailed and lose some momentum, but you need to recognize this and quickly get back to what is working. Think of it as being on a diet or in a good exercise routine. The holidays come around and throw you off track. How quickly can you return to the good habit? How easy will it be to maintain? As things pick up speed, people fail to recognize how hard it was to get to this pace. That's why you look to avoid people or projects that will impede momentum.

DBAS : Big audacious projects must be separated from your main business because they can sap momentum.

Big Moves Can Kill Momentum

Part of maintaining momentum is recognizing your limitations. Even though you must take advantage of when things are good, you mustn't overcommit yourself. Avoid doing things that don't fit your style. For example, massive hiring is going to force you from your natural path. This might seem like a good idea to hire a bunch of people, so you can grow fast. Yet that's going to take your focus away from what's been working. Most likely this will not allow you to grow with the same efficiency. Grow at a pace that is reasonable for your business overall and won't weigh down your positive momentum. Hyper growth often takes your eye off the ball.

Game Changing Deals

Be mindful of big deals, they can derail momentum. People work on a huge sale or a big new contract that will change the dynamics of the company. This can include mergers, the sale of the company or something like bringing on a new major client. It's easy to get seduced into what the company will look like if you seal the deal. This makes it easy to lose sight of measured progress. Just like in a major project, you must find a way to divorce yourself. Separate this deal from the day to day events.

Make Hay While the Sun is Shining

Another concept to think on, is that rinse and repeat of making money is a solid strategy. People often make things harder than they need to be. Or because things are going well, they feel the need to take giant leaps because they can. Times will get harder because that's just how the world works. Don't make that eventuality happen before it should.

The old saying "Make hay while the sun is shining" is part of momentum. If you've found something that works be aggressive about it. Make what you can, while you can. It's almost a guarantee that the window on the method that you're using will close. It's a little bit of Goldilocks. You don't want to overgrow but you don't want to undergrow. Momentum is equal to the natural speed of growth. Get going while the going is good.

DBAS: There is nothing wrong with making a profit doing the same thing over and over.

Gotcha: The Archenemy of Startups

Momentum is the good feeling of executing your plan, knowing yourself and moving forward at a natural pace. The opposite of momentum are things that I like to call gotcha's. (Some call them black swans but I'm not that fancy). Gotchas are simply things that you don't see coming. And for the most part you couldn't see coming. They will happen. Count on it.

Gotchas fall into a plethora of categories. Of course, I can't sit here and tell you that I know about every gotcha that's coming down the road. That's kind of the point of gotchas. They are hard to see and get camouflaged. When you do finally see them, it is too late to reverse their impact. You must employ your wit, grit and bullshit to not let them kill you.

I'd like to give you some examples of gotchas I've experienced through my career. You likely won't experience the exact same ones, but no matter the industry you're in, they're going to happen. Hopefully by hearing my stories will help you prepare for your own.

The hope is that they come at a time in which you will be able to overpower them. In a way that you will be able to utilize whatever happens to make your business stronger going forward. Learn from these situations so you don't have the same problem happen twice.

Government Gotcha

Let's start with the government. This usually has to do with taxes, licensing, zoning, regulation, permits etc. One that comes to mind is where we weren't filing the appropriate taxes for payroll. This was because we were operating in multiple states and certain territories needed additional forms where others didn't. We found out about a year down the road and it cost a bunch of money.

I've also had the government come after me about certification. In travel you need to be certified to operate in California and Florida. When I found out it surprised me because I had never heard of an explicit travel filing. This wasn't as simple as submitting a form and paying a fee. You had to have specific insurance and bonds. All stuff that sounds scary when you are blindsided by it. Also, the government is keen on showing your worst-case scenario on how much fines could be or even possible criminal prosecution. You must be careful. Some of this I could have seen coming. But we learned how to operate in one state and just assumed the rest of the country was the same.

DBAS: Assumption is at the heart of most avoidable gotchas.

The government can come back years later and fine you thousands of dollars for every error. If you made a thousand errors, you naturally freak out. You're going to figure out this mostly bluster. Get your accountant, lawyer or somebody to help you out. This a recurring theme, having a wise group of advisers around you. A strong network will shepherd you through the gotchas.

Acts of God

Another category of gotchas is an act of God. This relates to weather: hurricanes, tornadoes, snowstorms, pandemics anything along those lines. It depends on the type of business you're in. This could be something like an extended period of bad weather or a drought.

If you operate a jet ski rental place and it rains every weekend all summer that's not an act of God. More like a business where a tornado rips through your headquarters . Or your office gets flooded and your servers are wrecked. Taking you offline for an extended period. That's not something you could have easily foreseen. You should plan for unlikely things, but you can't plan for everything.

There are going to be times where an act of God will occur. You could be running a big sale one weekend or hosting a major event and it will snow, rain, tornado, whatever. Even if you have thought it through it will not be like you are operating normally. You can't control the weather. Triage and problem solve is what entrepreneurs do.

Geopolitical Gotchas: True Black Swans

There are two black swans that I have experienced that were caused by an event in the world outside of my control. They were 9/11 and the economic collapse of collapse 2008. During both these happenings I was in the travel industry. (As I write this, we are experiencing a 3rd. The Corona Virus pandemic, but Ill save that for the audio book. LOL)

Let's start with 9/11. This was a horrible tragedy and I had family living blocks away from ground zero. Luckily, they were spared. Being in the travel business our sales dropped significantly. Additionally we had writers and photographers traveling all over the US at the time. They were grounded and stranded because all planes were grounded. We had to figure out a way to house them, feed them and get them back safely. This took some patience by all involved but it worked out. One writer even ended up driving back to New Jersey from Las Vegas.

The business of selling travel just disappeared. For the first few days after 9/11 there were more cancellations than bookings. This had never happened in the history of travel agencies. Not just losing the potential revenue you would make, but giving back proceeds you made previously. Not something that you could have foreseen. We were both fortunate and unfortunate because our business had just started to take off. Hence, we were still sitting on enough reserves to make it through. Yet it stalled the steep growth curve we had been on.

This changed the travel industry climate for years and still has an impact on the business today.

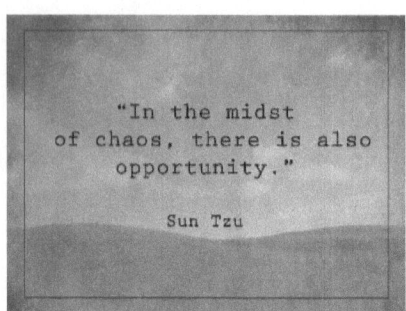

"In the midst of chaos, there is also opportunity."

Sun Tzu

Keep in mind that some black swans can turn into opportunities. What happened after 9/11 is the travel business got hurt so bad that hotels were empty. They needed a lot more help finding business. Companies were willing to do deals that they would never have considered before this tragic event.

9/11 was a big challenge for our company, but it also cleared the path for better deals with our suppliers and closer relationships with our partners. A crisis will bring people together.

Financial Meltdown

9/11 was not something that we could see coming in any way. The economic collapse of 2008 was not easily predicted either. You could somewhat see that we were in an economic bubble. The real estate market had been on an absurd uptrend and wise people assumed that couldn't continue. At the time, I was operating in a sector that required the consumers to use credit to make purchases. In 2008, over a matter of a few weeks the whole world's access to credit practically disappeared.

If you were selling something that involves credit you were in a lot of trouble. We were in the vacation ownership industry, which is tangentially related to the real estate. My business was sending perspective clients to the companies who sold vacation ownership. They would give us criteria of a person who they deemed financially qualified. (People making $40k a year and had a major credit card). After the meltdown they altered these parameters significantly, which narrowed the pool of people we could target by 50%. If you lop off half of your customer base in an instant, you're in for some rough times.

Even with hindsight it was hard to plot out that the world would suddenly go from anybody and everybody being able to get credit to absolutely nobody getting credit. It's not something that you could plan for because it hadn't happened before. The vacation ownership industry barely survived with many major companies going into bankruptcy protection.

Once the dust settled, just like 9/11 there were more opportunities in the market because the people who needed customers got creative. They changed the rules of the game. Finding new ways to secure people credit or requiring less money down. New products like travel clubs were invented to allow for higher margins and less financing.

If you hang in there, you will likely find opportunity. These events are horrible, but sometimes it's easier to navigate when the whole world bands together to find solutions. Whereas with internal gotchas you are on your own.

Side Tracked

Survive and advance is a mantra I have mentioned earlier. When these worldwide events happen, the result will be some companies go under. Just by staying alive, you will gain a leg up. When things turn around and they almost always do, you will have less competition.

Pesky Investors

Gotcha's can come from investors as well. This is can be like a civil war, where investors try to force you into certain actions. Gotchas with investors are different than standard disagreements. Usually this happens when there is a change in investors or if an investor has a change in their life. They may see a path for the company that better serves them than the one that you are following. It doesn't matter how big or small the investors are, they can all cause trouble.

A shareholder may have had a change in their income level and now wants to see their investment produce dividends immediately instead of the down the road. Be careful when you take on investors as I spoke of in the capital raising chapter. Make it clear what their rights are and how they can voice their opinions. Pesky investors can hold up major deals if they want to be a pain in the ass. It's a hell of a hindrance if you are about to sell your company, but an investor doesn't like the terms and tries to block the deal. The easiest way to keep investors from becoming gotchas is to keep regular contact with them and know what your shareholders agreement means.

Lawyers, Guns and Money

Lawsuits are often the source of unexpected problems. Customers can sue for basic reasons like a slip and fall or some similar liability. Competitors claim you stole their intellectual property . Suppliers can come after you for bidding on their keyword terms. These are just a few examples of the many types of issues people can claim. Try not to fear a lawsuit. I'm not saying that you shouldn't cause you concern, just don't wilt.

Anybody can sue anyone for anything.

The first time I got sued, I was 20 years old. Someone sued me for selling baseball cards and didn't like what they bought. I freaked out when I got a letter from a lawyer. I soon learned just because you get sued doesn't mean something bad will happen. Somehow, they ended up giving me the cards back and getting just a fraction of what they spent returned. I guess I had a good lawyer. But when I got that initial letter my imagination ran wild with all the bad things that could happen. You shouldn't ignore a lawsuit obviously, seek advice before slamming your head against a brick wall.

Another time, my company got sued by a multi-billion-dollar company because we wouldn't let them try and buy us. We were involved in negotiations with two other corporations for an acquisition and these guys didn't want to be left out. They sued us to try and throw a monkey wrench in the whole process. Didn't work, but it spooked me good and proper.

DBAS: Lawsuits are usually not the type of thing that you can flip and turn into your benefit. Accepting lawsuits as part of doing business will serve you well. Try and keep your emotions in check.

The Buck Always Stops Here: Like It or Not

Employee mistakes or missteps are another set of gotchas that I've dealt with over the years. I've worked on major projects for a year. Tracking progress the whole way through. Only at the end did I realize that there was a major flaw in the product. My employees either knowingly deceived me or were not giving me accurate information.

In one case we ended up with a product that was too slow for use on the open market. We had built something that was like Kayak years before they existed. One of the first meta travel engines. We called it the mother of all booking engines.

We had been testing it internally and it worked great. Yet when we went live the searches took three or four minutes to return travel results. The internal trials had functioned well because we were caching some of the results and not using 100% live data. The programmers had used enough live results that it appeared to be a real product, just enough to fool me during the development process. That made it appear faster and my team thought it worked.

The fact that they didn't reveal this information to us was the issue, the gotcha. Myself and other execs had asked a lot of questions and demanded we hit markers during development. There was no real way to double check the info I was getting from my team. I had to trust them. Regardless of who was at fault, I am to blame. Either I didn't ask the right questions, or I hired the wrong people. But I sure was blindsided by the result. In hindsight I think this might have cost me more in potential earnings than any other single gotcha.

Hidden in Plain Sight

Here is another instance where an employee's performance ended up causing a problem that hit me like a brick to the side of the head. Our in-house accountant was tracking sales and cancellations on sales. I said this in prior chapters where we had set a bar for 20 percent cancellations and it turned out they came in at 40+ percent. These cancellations were happening over the course of three to six months. We didn't see the effect of it till it was almost too late.

Our reports showed we were spending a dollar and bringing in a dollar twenty-five. Turns out we were bringing in seventy five cents for every dollar spent. When you think you're bringing in a 25% profit, you repeat the process as many times as you can. When it turns out that it was totally the opposite it has a major impact. Duh! The accountant wasn't matching the incoming revenue with the sales receipts from previous months. Hence the reports we were getting weren't accurate.

Since we were taking large deposits for future trips the cash position looked decent. Also, the main thing that was growing was our accounts receivable. The money we were owed was from a multibillion-dollar public company, hence we weren't worried about collecting that debt.

As it turned out the accounts receivable weren't growing as much as we thought. From the time of the sale till the time we were due to be paid averaged about 6 months. If the accountant had been reconciling the revenue properly, we would have seen red flags in the short term. By the time we figured it out we had almost bankrupted the company. I had a hired an accountant who had experience in the timeshare industry. Yet since we were doing something new, generating leads from the internet, his past familiarity turned out to be a negative. As I placed trust in someone who wasn't as knowledgeable about what we were doing as I thought.

Employee mistakes can steer you into an iceberg, but in the end you're always accountable for what your employees do. These were costly mistakes. There's no doubt that I could have done more, but you must trust your employees on some level. That's why it's so important to hire good people who have as much experience doing exactly what they're doing as possible.

You will hire some bad employees if you do it long enough and get big enough. They're going to cause problems, how you react and overcome is going to help define who you are as a person and as a business.

Suppliers Gonna Get You

Every day of your business there are going to be suppliers and vendors that you rely on to operate. You never know exactly what is going on inside these companies. They can throw some trouble at you from left field.

Another problem I have encountered are vendors changing terms on billing or payment. A vendor who was paying every 30 days like clockwork for years suddenly decided that they were going to switch to 90 days. That created a massive cash flow problem and we had to solve it without notice.

It wasn't like they were going out of business and were still our biggest vendor. You have to roll with the punches. Therefore, it's always good to have some reserves in the bank or have access to extra cash lined up just in case. Good advice I have been given is that the best time to get access to credit is when you don't need it.

DBAS: Get your suppliers to commit to payment terms in contracts and include a penalty for changing them.

On the other side, suppliers will increase prices without notice. Change terms of contracts. Or worse, decide to compete in the marketplace. When I was doing work with hotels.com selling on 5,000 websites they thought they were smarter than us. They decided to directly compete with what we were doing. They had been able to see our methods through their tracking system and attempted to duplicate it by producing thousands of small hotel websites. They failed, but it hurt our business and our relationship with them.

Another supplier who always seems to be changing the game without notice is Google. One day they decided to eliminate the right-side ads on their search engine results. They realized they were getting most of their money from ads on the top of the page. By creating greater scarcity for those ads, they could charge more money. This hurt our business because we had found a sweet spot on the right-hand side of their results that maximized profit. Suddenly it was gone. This change eliminated a lot of the competitors who couldn't make money anymore. I survived and thrived, but not without struggle.

Vendors and suppliers can change things and it's totally out of your control. You're not privy to their inner workings. You can't see the internal finances of somebody you're working with to know trouble is coming. Turn problems into learning and find new ways to finance, fight competitors and work with partners.

Banks and Credit Card Companies

Gotchas from banks and credit card companies are serious issues. In past chapters I detailed my issues with utilizing American Express to finance a business. They gave us an unlimited credit line and pulled it without notice.

Thieving Merchant Bastards

The credit line was an easier issue to see and avoid than the next one, merchant accounts. Those are the processors that allow you to take credit cards to make sales. Since all business on the internet and phone is done via credit card they are the conduit for all your money. A major issue with your credit card processor can bring your business to a halt. It's not like the service they provide comes cheap, they charge fees between 2-5% for this service. (Those fees are very negotiable over time and go up and down on a mélange of factors.)

What I didn't realize is that these merchant account credit card companies sometimes will require a deposit. The deposit is used in case you sell goods and don't provide them to the customers. Then they can refund them. Not only can they require a deposit, but they can change the amount that they require at any time. If that wasn't bad enough, the method they will use to collect this deposit is to start keeping the money you are charging your customers. Which means without much notice the money you are expecting to go into your bank account from sales gets diverted to them for a deposit. WTF.

One November our merchant account provider came to us and said we need a $200,000 deposit to continue using them. Now I didn't have a free 200K to throw at this. Before we could even respond they started taking the money from every transaction that we processed. A hundred percent of our transactions were via credit card. None of the money from our sales was coming to our account. There was no point in making sales because we didn't get the money. From a cash flow perspective, it was as if we were giving everything away for free. If we didn't fix this, we would go out of business fast.

Immediately we scrambled to set up a different merchant account that wouldn't require that type of deposit. It's one thing for them to say they needed a deposit, but no notice and such a large figure were what really hurt. We had never had any issues or problems with them, but they suddenly decided that the travel industry was risky.

What some people don't realize is that merchant accounts are lending you money. They are giving you money based on services you deliver at a later date. In reality, they wanted to make sure we didn't charge people for vacations that happened in six months and in the meantime run off with the money. Since we were honest people this never occurred to us. In hindsight what they did was completely reasonable, but only once I realized how we could have screwed people if we were evil.

For a week or two we used PayPal to do our transactions, they charged double our standard merchant fees. We were lucky that we had set this up for something entirely unrelated. It kept us afloat for the time it took to find a new merchant who didn't require a significant deposit.

It's a big challenge, you don't expect somebody to suddenly massively change the terms that you've been operating with for a long time. An item which is literally the life blood of your company. The fix for this is always have a backup merchant account or at least a backup merchant account plan that you can put into place if you run into trouble. I began by saying there are gotchas that hopefully I can help you avoid and others that nobody could. Merchant accounts are one that you have been warned about now and should be prepares to solve.

Sidetracked: Chargebacks

As you can see on the internet these merchant accounts can completely control you. Small business gets the shaft when it comes to chargebacks too. A chargeback is where somebody says they bought your product, but didn't get what they paid for. The customer calls their credit card company to dispute the charge and asks for their money back. This would be fine if people were reasonable and honest but guess what they are not.

With small businesses credit card companies don't give a crap about you. You are guilty until proven innocent. They require you to provide proof that you delivered your product perfectly. This sounds easy, but when someone is lying it can be hard to disprove a negative. Whereas when a customer tries to dispute a charge against big business, getting your money back is a struggle. These merchants protect their big clients and leave the small ones out to dry.

An example, my favorite aunt booked a cruise, months in advance and when the time came to go a hurricane was headed in their path. The cruise company knew about this and that there were going to be massively high seas. Did they cancel it? Nope. 80 percent of the people got sick including my poor aunt. When she got home, she tried to get a refund. The credit card company said no because the cruise line was a substantial customer.

On the flipside of this, a little company had booked somebody in a hotel room and the customer found a hair in the bathroom. This person then calls their credit card company after staying in the hotel room for four days and complains about the hair. They demand a full refund and the card company instantly opens a dispute. Somehow the little company now must prove that there wasn't a hair in the bathroom. Some unsavory people count on businesses not taking the time to fight these chargebacks. People suck and when you're a little guy the credit card companies do not look out for you.

Final Words

That's my take on momentum and gotchas. The key with momentum is simply that you must guard it. You can't take it for granted and must look out for anything that's going to diminish your momentum.

Gotcha's are the boogeyman of owning your own business. For the most part having experience and controlling your emotions is what will save you from the fear. Grit will see you through. Having cash reserves along with a well established corporate shield is a good idea. Solid advisers and a good network are also key in overcoming these black swans.

DBAS: How you guard your momentum and react to gotcha's could very well define your business. You got this.

Chapter 25: Failure is a Part of Life

Failure: Be ready for it. Never like it. Always learn from it.

Understand that gotcha's and failure are completely different. Gotchas are when something comes out of the blue that you couldn't have foreseen. Failure is when you didn't reach your goals because you didn't execute your plan due to your own errors. Failure can be compartmentalized or can be total. Complete failure is when you are forced out of business. Other failures are ones that are limited to specific segments of your business.

Don't equate quitting with failure. People are taught to never give up. That's a nice platitude, but quitting is sometimes the best move. Quitting is a part of an entrepreneur's life. They will try a lot of stuff and if it doesn't pan out best to quit. We soften this move by saying we are pivoting. Don't get hung up on it. Life is the war everything else is the battle. Never give up the overall fight, but it's not only ok, but necessary to cut your losses in some spots.

Not many people want to prepare you for failure. They are afraid that their ego can't accept the concept.

DBAS: You're not going to be undefeated in life. Take failure like a champ.

Be Prepared to Take a Punch

A way to avoid failure is to be ready to take a punch. Leave yourself a little extra room for error. Extra money in the bank can always help mitigate failure.

Looking to make sure you have balance or diversity in revenue streams make you stronger and capable to absorb more problems. If you only have one source that makes you money and it goes away, you're going to be in trouble.

That's Pride Fucking with You

Do not be too proud to admit that you've failed. Pride comes before the fall they say. People like to think that they're smart and there is no possible way that they could have failed. They look for scapegoats or excuses. Blame isn't your friend. The people who are most successful in this world accept responsibility for mistakes and learn from them. Identify the problem, even if it was a simple dumb mistake by you and own it.

Sometimes you won't see the breakdown right away. It will be in the result, in the final number. Then you do the detective work to figure out exactly where the problem was. Is there a specific weak link or was it more of a systematic issue? Then cut it out and move on. If you get too caught up in the fact that there was a failure you make it worse. Balance recognizing the failure with not miring in it.

Solving Problems Versus Being Right.

This distinction is a core lesson in how to be an effective person and leader. When you fail at something, too many arguments are about rehashing prior opinions. So, people can be seen as being right or correct. Not enough focus is put on solving the problem. People who want to win an argument and ignore how to address the problem will always be less effective. These are people you should look to educate or remove from your life.

DBAS: There is little value in being "right" after the fact. Be concerned mainly with solving the problem.

Failure Into Opportunity

Has your business failed or has something you're doing in your business failed? The distinction is whether there is a place in which you can pivot.

Failure can be an opportunity. The opportunity can come by doing that detective work. In examining the process, you will see not only what failed, but also what worked. In my web travel guide businesses we were failing in the first year. Producing and operating these guides was burning cash. Sending writers and photographers out to cities was costly. The advertising money just wasn't paying the bills.

Then we looked closely at the traffic on our sites to find out if there was a way to cut costs. Focusing more on what people were interested in and removing what wasn't important. We found that users were spending more time in the hotel section than anywhere else. The content for hotels came from a partner and was free to us. We also were making more money from hotel referrals than from advertising. So instead of building travel guides which were expensive we started to build hotel sites that were far cheaper. Bingo. 5 times the revenue at a tenth of the cost.

What was an early failure of not being able to get advertisers or produce travel guides efficiently turned into a very successful business. Creating hotel sites was a lucrative enterprise that ran for many years. Companies pivot all the time. They do this because they have failed at something but see opportunity elsewhere. If we had tunnel vision and refused to see this opening we likely would have gone out of business.

Examining your failure and looking for the bright spots is where some of the best things will come from. That's why you can't get too overwhelmed by missing the mark. People who can pivot and move in different directions will do well. Be nimble. Don't overcommit to a project or path until you are certain. If you leave yourself a little wiggle room you increase your chances of turning failure into success.

DBAS: Failure can often be turned into victory if you have enough resources to pivot.

Limiting Exposure

Limiting your exposure in failure is mostly about how you went about setting up the company. Whose money did you use? Corporate structure? Investors? Etc. (Obviously if it's a failure the less money of yours the better. This is covered in the raising capital chapter. Hindsight is 20/20 and no one sets out to fail).

Having a solid corporate structure is important in bad times. If you're running some sort of partnership or sole proprietorship you can open yourself up to extended liability. Like negligence or other potential lawsuits. Therefore, it makes more sense to set up as an LLC or corporation. The risk is just too high for little reward in other structures.

Corporate Structure

Which One is Right For You?

Type of Company	Administration	Easy Tax	Liability	Raising Capital
Sole Proprietor	Good	Good	Bad	Bad
LLC	OK	Good	Good	OK
S Corporation	Bad	Bad	Very Good	Good
C Corporation	Bad	Bad	Very Good	Very Good

Don't Bury Your Head in the Sand

What I've found is that when it comes to failures most of your investors and partners understand there is risk. What you must do is manage expectations. Good communications with the investors and the stockholders will help limit your exposure if failure comes. You don't want to hide your failure, but you can spin it. Be honest about what's happened. But you can also highlight the positives or where the company is going in the future.

What is Your Helm's Deep?

One useful tactic when facing failure, I borrowed from The Lord of the Rings. When attacked on all sides this group of people would fall back to their stronghold. They would retreat to an impenetrable place called **Helm's Deep**.

Legend was they could last for generations there. Weather the storm of any attack. That concept perfectly describes one way to survive rough times. In case of failure you should have a Helm's Deep for yourself and your business. A place that lets you stay afloat and live to fight another day.

Storms are going to come, and you can stem the tide of full-blown complete failure. You retreat not out of cowardice, but because you recognize standing and fighting will lead to your doom. Without this fallback point you would no longer exist.

Have a Helm's Deep strategy. Create it in your mind, a safe place that you can retreat . One that's not entirely pleasurable but where you can survive. By place I mean level of operation. How could you cut costs if need be? There are certain expenses in life where once you commit to them it's hard to get out of them. If you buy a house with a huge mortgage it's going to take time to turn into cash or eliminate that monthly outlay. If you spend a lot of money each week on food or your cable bill that you can cut back immediately.

What can you or your business live on? Think of a life raft with limited space and how you'd supply it. If you only have so much you can pay for what exactly is that going to be? There will be employees that are essential to your existence and others that you could live without. There was a time where I scaled a business back from 50 people to 2 just to keep the lights on. We pivoted and scaled back up. Helm's Deep was our salvation.

DBAS: Sometimes the right move might be to start a new company. If all that is left is debt, yet you still own the ideas start over. A fresh entity. Psychology and logically it's the smart decision.

Half Empty or Half Full

Planning for failure is not something you should do daily. Yet in the back of your mind have a plan where if it rained shit on you, this is what I'm going to do. It's easier to execute a plan that exists than if you make it up as you go. Some people are reasonable about planning for failure and not necessarily as good about planning for success. Depends on the individual.

By their nature realists are more likely to have plans for failure and dreamers are more prone to prepare for success. Try to be equal parts of both. Those inner demons fight each other, but as a good businessperson you should have the dreamer and the realist inside of you. Neither should dominate. Balanced, humble, nimble.

"It's not how many times you get knocked down that count, it's how many times you get back up." George S. Custer

---

One Failure Shouldn't End You

Failure happens to everybody. Learn from failure. But don't let it scar you. A child grabbing onto the handle of the hot pot gets burned. It is a way they learn and then don't do it again. When it comes to business sometimes, you're going to gamble and roll snake eyes. If you lose that ability inside to take a risk, then you're out of the game. Everybody's going to get knocked down. They're going to take an L. You got to keep going.

Odds and Variance

I'm preaching balance, learn from your failures but you can't let them drive all your decisions. In the future not everything is going to be a failure. There's variance in life and you could have just been unlucky. (Don't use this as an excuse for failure, but it could be an explanation).

Say you had a set of dice and the outcome of the roll determined your success. In this case you only fail if you roll two sixes, which is thirty-five to one. If you roll two sixes right out of the gate and you lost all your money you'd be scarred by the outcome. Yet 35 out of 36 times you were going to win. You can't look at that one small sample of failure to drive your entire life. Know the odds and know variance will occur.

DBAS: Sometimes you just get unlucky. Don't give up.

Final Words:

Failure is a part of the game. If you are not failing you are not trying enough. Prepare for bad times. Sometimes just surviving is a victory. At the end of it, get over failure. Pick yourself up, dust yourself off, and get back in the game. Remember shooters shoot.

Chapter 26: Success. Are You Ready?

Let's talk about success, that's a good part of starting a business. Hitting the goals you laid out when you started. Yet it's not always exactly what you thought it would be and can be helpful to examine it closer. You must prepare for success just like you would failure.

People are so worried about limiting the downside that they aren't prepared for the upside. This may seem ridiculous to you right now, but there are some pitfalls and new responsibilities that come along with success.

This is Worth Repeating: Make Hay

I said it before I'll say it again make hay while the sun is shining. You struck oil, but the world is going to change and what works today won't last forever. Get as much out of it as you can for as long as you can. It's likely that you will have pockets of success and regression. Maximize the good times and minimize the bad ones.

There are ads I come across every day that say make $200,000 a year with your own business. Of course, I know these claims are mostly false. Yet I think, if a person is able to hit that mark how long will it last? If you hit that mark for one year but are bust the next was that a success? The goal isn't to make a certain amount of money in a year, it is to be financially secure and independent

Money is here. Now what?

Know what to do with your new-found money when you get it. Are you a person that knows how to invest? Some people are great at making money, but they have no idea how to manage or invest it. They focus on how they are going to spend their riches , but don't consider growing wealth.

Long term/ short term. I'm not going to sit here and tell you how to invest your money, but you should find people who have extensive knowledge on the topic. Depending on your age or your ultimate goals that's how you know whether you should be aggressive or not. Stocks, index funds, real estate, bonds etc. Learn a little about each and see if there is one that appeals to you. Even if you hand your money over to a financial advisor, knowing enough that you can't be bullshitted will help you sleep better at night.

Don't just think now that you've got this sum of money that the game is over. Think about financial security and freedom. Those are the goals which come with the greatest reward in terms of happiness.

Don't Count Anyone Else's Money

Never count another person's money. Worry about what you have and not someone else's bank account. Whether the successes come from operations, through a sale or some sort of other means keep focus on what you have made. Don't concern yourself with somebody else.

I've seen too many people in teams/partnerships where once they've achieved success, they start looking over their shoulder and seeing how their peers are being rewarded. One partner might have gotten in earlier or they might be more important to the business. Don't worry about it. Focus on your happiness because there's always going to be somebody with more money than you. Judging your success by how others do is a bottomless pit.

Of course, you want things to be fair but avoid sour grapes because somebody else got more. There's probably somebody else who might be upset because you got what you did.

DBAS: True happiness isn't found by judging your success relative to others.

Enjoy it!

"When you achieve success, the best thing to do is enjoy it." I know it's a cliché but stop and smell the roses. Some get so lost in the pursuit that they don't take a moment to recognize their achievement.

Success won't last, but who cares. Even if you continue being successful there will be a peak. In life everything is relative. People get caught up in trying to push further and further in the business and lose sight of their original goals.

Remember why you said you wanted to do this in the first place. Now that you have achieved success what is the next step? When first discussing goals for starting a business we recognized that financial reward does not equate to happiness. Now that you have reached the mountain top it's time to reexamine those goals.

Side Note: Once you get success, take care of things that you let lapse. Your teeth, your house, your physical fitness, strayed friendships, love life, hobbies. We sacrifice a lot to achieve our business goals, now is the time to try and catch up on those things that we have let slip.

The Thrill of the Climb

Here's another cliché, the journey really is the best part. It's so true and it's unfortunate because you can never capture the journey. The journey is your life. The journey was the ride up to this point and achieving success. If it's a long-term success, where you're continuing to operate, continuing to grow that's different than if you've achieved some sort of liquidity event. One where you're getting out of the business. That journey would have ended.

If you are still involved and have assed your goals again, you can try to keep going. Hold on to it as long as you can, enjoy it. Your next project might be a failure, so soak it all in.

I'd Like to Thank the Academy

Take time to appreciate the team and the people that helped you get to your goals. This is sounding like an Academy Award speech but that is ok. You need to show the people on your team, your family or whoever it is that you are grateful for their support.

You could throw a party and invite everybody. Doesn't need to be extravagant, just because you've achieved some level of financial success you don't need to be wasteful or flaunt it. (That would produce the opposite of your goal). At the party make a speech from your heart that says how these people are important to you. Let them know you realize their impact on your life and thank them.

Instead of a party you could buy gifts. Again, it's not necessarily about the dollars you spend but the thought and the care that you put into it. The more you can personalize something the better. That doesn't mean going out and buying your group of friends each a different color Ferrari. This is about understanding who they are as individuals. Show how you feel and just spending money does not necessarily equate with appreciation. Thoughtfulness and care show you are truly grateful. People who only appreciate something because it's expensive or audacious probably are never going to be happy with what you get them anyway.

Haters Gonna Hate

This leads me to another part of dealing with success. Be careful who you let know about your success. In this world of social media and constant PR, there's a benefit to building your brand around success. Yet, there are going to be haters, people who just don't like you because you've succeeded. That's something that's hard to accept. People don't like you because you accomplished something and no other reason.

Success likely didn't come easy to you. You sacrificed. You did a lot of things other people are unwilling to do. People will hate you, there's no way around that. You're just going to have to zone them out and not let it affect you. Don't let it change you from who you are. You can't win them over.

And there'll be gossip. Depending on the level of your success or where you live, people will talk. I'm sure there are some smaller social circles within your larger circles. There'll be chatter about your success and a lot of it won't be true. I've heard rumors about myself over time; how much money I made or deals I turned down; deals I've done; personal relationships, money I've spent, things I've bought, people I've screwed over. Almost none of it was true. I found it funny because the legend becomes more interesting than the truth. Know this will happen and try to laugh it off best you can.

DBAS: Envy is a sign of success. Its not fun, but not much you can do about it. Being self-deprecating is the best defense.

Keep the Details Private

Be careful about letting actual numbers get out in the public. You don't need others to know the details of your success. There'll be ways to hide your financial success and I think this is better than letting your ego get the better of you. Just don't talk numbers period. I don't care if it's your family or friends. Other people will begin to make assumptions based off of numbers if they know them. It's better to just talk in generalities like "doing really well" "I'm very comfortable financially" or "a place that allows me freedom". Statements like those instead of "hey I made a million dollars last year or this deal was worth ten million dollars to me." Those are not good things to put out into public. They can only serve to hurt you in the future.

To just volunteer personal financial information to anyone is a bad idea. This usually happens with younger people, they seek an exalted place in society that they think money brings. Keep your cards close to your vest unless there is something directly to be gained.

Your Ego and No New Friends

Success will bring another group of people to you, the hangers on. They are kind of the opposite of the haters but can be more dangerous. Don't surround yourself with sycophants, people who just say yes. People are attracted to winners. They want to be around individuals who have achieved and, on some level, envy you. Some feel like that your Golden Touch is going to rub off on them.

There's a good chance that they will just yes you to death. "Yes" people are of no value to you at any stage of your life. There's a difference between people being supportive and just saying yes. Those being supportive may not say something every time they see you doing something wrong. Yet, if you're headed down a dark path, a true friend will try to steer you in the right direction. Sycophants will carry your bags on the way to hell.

Don't spend your well-earned coin on those who don't care about you. I've made this mistake when I was young and single. Going out to nightclubs and spending large sums of money on bar tabs for big groups of people. For a few years, anybody I met I would buy a drink, a meal or whatever. As I got wiser, I realized this approach wasn't having the desired impact. I wanted to share the wealth and be a walking party. This attracts the wrong type of people.

There are strategic ways to blow off some steam and spend a few bucks. I'm not telling you to be cheap, just be value oriented. Don't feel like you need to spend money just because you can or to show others that you have it. Even if the desired effect is to attract attention it's much better if that info seeps out slowly. Don't hit people over the head with your success.

People say "you can't buy friends", but you can rent them. These people are usually shallow, and give you the same feeling as eating fast food. Good when you do it, but you're going to regret it later. Be mindful of the people you surround yourself with and who you are spending your money on. It is ok to have fun, just don't run away with the circus.

Check Yourself

The next part of dealing with success is just controlling your ego. Now that you've achieved, it's very easy to get overconfident. There's a fine line between cockiness and confidence. You want to stay confident, but while

299

remaining humble. If you show me somebody who's not humble, you are showing me somebody who is about to be humbled. I've been humbled many times and I've learned from it.

Over the years you get scarred, but this is what helps you learn to control your ego. Simply remember there is always somebody out there with more than you, that did it better than you. This isn't belittling your success. It is just reminding you that you shouldn't base your whole existence on it.

You set out to do something and you achieved it. It's hard not to feel your own hype right now but be true to yourself. Some elements of your success were likely due to luck. That's OK. It's ok to accept this because the harder you work the luckier you are. I'd always rather be lucky and good. So maybe don't pound your chest too hard. Just be thankful.

You were in the right place at the right time. That's great because that's what you need to do in life, if you put yourself out there sometimes you fail, sometimes you succeed. That's the point of this. Don't believe because you succeeded that nobody else ever could have done this or that you're so amazing. Did you cure cancer? Check yourself. Not because what you did wasn't an amazing achievement, but because that feeling of heightened ego won't serve your long-term happiness.

I'm not trying to be Buzz Killington. My goal is to get you to be self-aware. So, if your ego has taken over your life, you will see it and be able to walk it back.

DBAS: A lot of successful people become their own worst enemies, and this is usually due to ego.

Determine Your Level

There are levels of financial success and I like to break it down into three main categories. First is where you have what you want for today. Meaning I want for nothing today more than I have. I call this "now money". The other end of the spectrum is "fuck you money" which I'm sure you've heard before. Fuck you money means nobody can tell you what to do. This is enough money that you never have to work again and be able to pay for whatever you want out of life.

After a successful run in business a lot people fall into the first two categories. Those are the easiest to navigate because one you must keep going and the other you don't. The last category is what I call "I'll figure it out money" That's in the middle, where you don't have enough money where you never have to work again. Yet you have enough cash that if you stop working you can take a while to figure out what is next.

On this level, look at yourself from where you are on that sliding scale of success financially. How long could you go without having to work before you start to feel pressure? The answer dictates how you look at things going forward.

Once you determine which category you are in then you can examine other aspects of your life to decide what's next.

Are you Still in Love with Your Company?

Examine your business because they change just like you did as a person. Your role may go from somebody who is building, growing, and pushing to one of just a caretaker. The business may have hit a point where there aren't new frontiers to chase down and it's on autopilot. You have become more of a babysitter instead of an innovator. That may not be who you want to be.

Ask yourself are you somebody who could sit on the beach all day and do nothing? Or do you live for the thrill of the hunt? Reevaluate the whole process and where your business can go. Is it something that you can take to a different level? And is that where you want to go, or would you rather just be on the beach and watch the money roll in. All are fine. It's just a matter of trying to set the direction you want to go versus just letting it happen to you.

Are You a Paul or a Bill?

Early on you will need to be indispensable and entirely irreplaceable, but that time has passed. Now you must decide whether you want that to continue. A lot of founders are visionaries who are the locomotives that drive their companies and then you have people who are going to jettison along the way. An extreme example would be Microsoft's Paul Allen and Bill Gates. Paul Allen was there early on for about 10-12 years and then because of health concerns he left never to return. After which he was known more for owning the Seattle Seahawks, the Portland Trailblazers and Vulcan ventures.

Bill Gates was the locomotive of Microsoft for its first 30 years. Well past the point of it being about the money Mr. Gates was the visionary of the company. There may come a point where you decide it's no longer about money. Would you rather be Paul Allen or would you rather be Bill Gates? If you ask me, I think Paul Allen was a much happier guy. Yet Gates has turned into the world's biggest philanthropist. But that's for you to decide.

DBAS: Be who you are, not who you'd wish you were.

Take a Break

If you are bored or burnt out I would tell you to consider a mini-retirement. Years ago, I read the book The Four-Hour Work Week. Tim Ferris has become quite popular with a huge following and a top podcast.

One big takeaway from the book I got was the concept of mini retirements. Instead of saving your money your whole life to retire at 60-65 you take breaks periodically throughout your career to re-examine your life and enjoy it. When you're 65 or whatever your target age is you may not have the physical vitality that you have as a young person. Plus, tomorrow is promised to no one. Some people save their whole life for a retirement they may never reach.

I've taken a few mini retirements, for example I played semi- professional poker for two years. I learned a lot during that process. This isn't something that most people have the option to explore, but at this point you have succeeded and you fall into this select group. It's definitely worth the thought. You should have some sort of focus or hobby because doing absolutely nothing can get old fast.

Final Words: Quality of life is the most important thing. Your success is meant to increase this. I hope that the achievement that you've come to through your business is fulfilling. Many people find that once they get where they want to be it's not as overwhelmingly positive as they thought it would be. I can't say this enough, financial success does not equate to happiness. It brings a level of comfort and security. Some people learn this too far down the road and it causes them to spiral. This won't be you because you are not a schmuck.

Making money can be addictive. If you have achieved X success before that becomes the floor of your next venture. It shouldn't be. Each adventure should be judged on its own and not in comparison to others.

Success is something to manage just like anything else in the process. In truth the journey, the struggle is where the fun is and that's why you want to consider starting another adventure. When I get to this point in the business or any fork in the road I think of one of my favorite TV shows, The

West Wing. Martin Sheen played president Jed Bartlett, when he was done with any topic he would just say "what's next?" That was his way of saying we're done with this and we're moving on. That's something that I would pose to you. Now that you have succeeded "what's next?"

Chapter 27: I Am Not a Role Model.

There was a famous Nike advertising campaign in the late 80s early 90s starring the basketball player Charles Barkley where he professed "I am not a role model". Meaning people should not pattern their lives after him even though he was successful.

I would say the same thing about myself. I'm not a role model and the point of this book is not for you to follow it step by step. I am just a guy who did a bunch of stuff, was involved in a lot of businesses over the years. I spend time self-assessing and looking back at the things that I did right and wrong. Why they happened the way they did. Some by chance. Some by architecture.

"I stand on the shoulders of giants"

There is No One Path

I built my life with the help of all the people that have come before me. All the books I read and all the businesses I studied, you can do the same. You can stand on the shoulders of giants. My story is unique and is yours. There is no one path, no matter what you read, what you learn or where you get your advice from. There isn't one way to do something. The people who've done best in the world recognize that and blaze their own trail.

Find Voices That Speak to You

Learn from the people before you but go your own way. Advice can be valuable or detrimental based on the person you are and who's giving the guidance. If you tell somebody to risk it all and they've got five kids and three ex-wives, it's different than telling that to somebody who is 21 years old and from a wealthy background. It's easier for some to roll the dice.

Advice affects people differently at different times of their lives. If you're looking to learn from others there will be many voices to choose from. Find a few that you trust and then buy into them. Experts aren't able to tell you everything you need to know, but some people's technique will resonate with you better than others. Pick the people that speak to you best and try to learn from them, you'll know them when you find them.

I have failed plenty and I've succeeded plenty as well. Anybody who wants to talk to you about a life that has no failure or downtimes is just selling you something. Trying to fool you that things are easy. Nothing of value is effortless .

DBAS: No one has all the answers.

My Wishes For You

There's a balance in this world that is the nature of things. Finding the balance that works for you is important. I have found it's much better to live with disappointment than regret. I'd rather do something and get a negative result than not do it and think what could have been.

The goal of this book is to keep you from making boneheaded moves. There is no universal advice. There are some overarching truths. I have tried to hammer them home and make them simple, so you don't end up being a schmuck. It's just that simple.

There are a helpful hints and moves in these pages. Science, math, strategies and techniques that you may be able to take and apply to your business. Then hopefully turn that into a pile of gold. That is certainly my hope. But usually the answer to any philosophical question is within you. By reading a book like this it's putting words to a feeling that you already have.

My goal is to keep you from making the mistakes that I've made, that I easily could see after the fact. They were tougher to see when I was in the heat of the battle and I want to remind you of the simple advice to stay humble, nimble, and curious. If you can do those things to the best of your ability, you will be able to roll with the punches. Be able to enjoy new horizons, get out of jams, and appreciate success and failure.

Happy over Money. Preferably Both

It's important to think through would you rather be Bill Gates or Paul Allen. Would you rather be Steve Jobs or Steve Wozniak. Would you rather be the guy that everybody remembers for running the company and having a hundred billion dollars or the guy who had fun with 20 billion dollars? I would always rather be the latter. There's only so much you can eat, so much you can drink. There are only so many cars you can drive, clothes you can wear, or houses you can live in. Focus on happy before money and you will be ok.

Final Final Words:
Success is Only Defined By You

I'll leave you with this last thought. I often say "you cannot tell someone else how to be happy". Which in turn means no one can define success for you. This you must do for yourself and do not let others impose their version of it upon you. It is key that the mountain you are trying to climb is of your own making.

With all that said I will tell you this: Good luck and please don't be a schmuck.